# THE BOOK OF
# Jewish Cooking

# THE BOOK OF
# *Jewish Cooking*

DENISE PHILLIPS

PHOTOGRAPHED BY
# DAVID MURRAY

PUBLISHED BY
SALAMANDER BOOKS LIMITED
LONDON

Published by Salamander Books Limited
8 Blenheim Court, Brewery Road, London N7 9NT

9 8 7 6 5 4 3 2 1

© Salamander Books Ltd., 2001

A member of the Chrysalis Group plc

ISBN 1 84065 217 9

Project managed by: Stella Caldwell
Editor: Madeline Weston
Designer: Mark Holt
Photographer: David Murray
Photographer's Assistant: Jules Selmes
Home Economist: Lizzie Harris
Filmset and reproduction by: Studio Tec, England
Printed in Spain

# CONTENTS

# FOREWORD

*In loving memory of my wonderful husband, Michael Phillips, who inspired and encouraged me to write this book. This book is also dedicated to my fabulous children, Abbie, Samantha and Nicholas for their patience, continuous support and love.*

I would like to thank Simone Leboff, who has been a friend and partner for many years, for her help putting this book on disc and for her hours of typing, advice, comments and assistance at cookery school. I would also like to thank another close friend, Marsha Schultz, who helped to edit the recipes and copy. Between them both, I have had someone to call on morning, noon and night about an idea or experiment. Their understanding husbands deserve a worthy mention, Roger and Martin respectively, because they have been there to provide child care whilst their wives have been working with me.

No book is a success without marketing and financial input and a big thank you to my cherished friends, Michael and Susan Hutter, for their effort in this area. I am very proud of my good friend, Lynne Misner, for writing a computer programme especially for me, and greatly appreciate all her help with the book.

Many thanks go to Salamander Books and their editing team, to David Murray and Jules Selmes for the photography, and to Liz Harris for being my food economist.

I have an extremely supportive family – parents, in-laws, and sisters. There is no doubt that I could not have achieved this book without their love and encouragement. My extended family in New York made me very welcome on my business trips and I am very grateful for their hospitality.

I have received much comfort and spiritual support from Rabbi Brawer for which I am eternally grateful. A thank you to Rebbetzin Dina Brawer whose contributions on Kashrut have been invaluable.

Eric Treuville, of Books for Cooks believed from day one that I had a great idea. He also introduced me to the right people in the publishing world for which I am very grateful.

Lastly, my 'guinea pig' friends, I thank you for your constructive comments and hope that you enjoyed my experimental dishes.

# INTRODUCTION

Cooking should be a fun and pleasurable experience, not a mad eleventh hour panic. In my view it is important to plan ahead and organise yourself, from the recipe list to the garnish and choice of wine. The following comprises a list of general tips for the cook along with notes on the recipes found in this book, as well as advice on planning and presentation to help create an air of effortless style.

Before starting to cook, doing the following two things will make your task much easier. First, thoroughly read through both the list of ingredients and the method, including timing information and alternatives. Second, locate and have everything you will need ready in advance. Having the correct ingredients to hand and measured makes the whole experience much faster and more efficient.

### INGREDIENTS
All ingredients are kosher. Some milky dishes may be made 'Parev' (food which contains neither meat or milk products) by substituting ingredi-

ents detailed in the recipes. Dishes suitable for Passover are indicated, as are any substitute ingredients.

• Always use fresh, organic produce where possible, as this will give the best flavour. If fresh herbs are not available, dried or frozen ones can be substituted in cooked dishes, but halve the quantities.

• Large eggs should be used, unless otherwise stated.

• Use unsalted butter, unless otherwise stated.

• To season, use sea salt and freshly ground pepper. Always taste before serving.

• All spoon measurements should be level, unless otherwise stated.

## GENERAL COOKING TIPS

• When pre-heating the oven, always turn it on at a temperature higher than you need. The minute you open the door the temperature drops. But do remember to heat the oven to the right temperature once the dish is in.

• Rearrange the oven trays to the appropriate depth and number of shelves before you turn the oven on. Moving them around when hot can be tricky. In addition, the longer the door is open the more heat you lose.

• Use base heat where possible. This means heating up a baking tray on

which you will place your food or dish. This speeds up the cooking process, as very few ovens have completely constant, all-round temperatures.

• When cracking an egg, if a piece of shell accidentally falls into the bowl, use another piece of shell to retrieve it. The egg shell acts as a magnet – this is much quicker than chasing it around with a spoon.

• When inviting your guests to eat with you, check out strong dislikes or allergies. This prevents you wasting time on something they can't eat and saves their embarrassment.

• Seasoning is a very important part of cooking; I always suggest tasting at the end before adding that extra sprinkling of salt and pepper. Flavours develop and change throughout the cooking process. In particular, too much salt at the beginning can spoil the final result or prevent the true flavours of the specific ingredients from coming through.

• Every now and then go shopping when you are not in a rush and browse

at the shelves you normally whizz past. New ingredients and ideas can be really inspiring – just go more slowly!

## THE GOLDEN RULES OF PRESENTATION

• Keep it simple – over-garnished or elaborately decorated food rarely appeals.

• Keep it fresh – nothing looks more off-putting than tired food.

• Keep it relevant – a sprig of fresh watercress complements lamb cutlets perfectly. The texture, taste and colour all enhance the lamb. However, scratchy sprigs of parsley, although providing colour, do not highlight the lamb and are unpleasant to eat.

## TRICKS OF PRESENTATION

• Centre height: Stacking certain foods to create a finished dish with height can turn the ordinary into something very special. For example, Aubergine Schnitzel (*page 67*) is layered, creating an aesthetically pleasing tower of colour.

• Contrasting rows: Biscuits, petit fours and canapés look

good arranged in neat rows. Combine one or two complementary colours and vary tastes and textures to create appetising and appealing food.

• Variety: Each mouthful should have a good combination of texture and flavour. Think carefully about the blend of different textures, tastes and flavours.

• Diagonal lines: Diamond shapes and diagonal lines are easier to achieve than straight ones.

• Dust: Dusting a plate with savoury paprika pepper or sweet icing sugar or cocoa powder gives an elegant finishing touch.

• Colour planning: The colour of food can be as important as the taste. Combine with care using matching or contrasting food and tableware. Black and white plain crockery dishes do not detract from food, whilst patterned plates could spoil the finished effect.

• Contrasting the simple and the elaborate: If the dish or bowl is elaborately decorated, simple foods will show off the design to the best effect.

• Uneven numbers: As a rule, use uneven numbers for the display of food. As with flower arranging, this has more appeal to the eye.

• A balanced look: Do not be mean – serve a generous portion, but avoid over-filling plates to use everything up. This can be messy and off-putting. It is better to leave that little bit extra off the plate, rather than cram it on – your guests can always return for more.

• Overlapping: Sliced meats, steaks, terrines, etc. look best evenly overlapping, and more can be fitted comfortably onto the plate.

• Best side uppermost: Usually the side of meat or fish which has been grilled or fried first should be presented uppermost. Bones are generally unsightly and if they can not be clipped off or removed, should be tucked away out of sight.

• Witty foods: It can be amusing and attractive to produce food which raises a smile or intrigues the diner. Try a sparkler in the Chocolate Baked Alaskas (page 86) as a spectacular finale to a dinner party.

# POTATO SKINS

baby new potatoes (3 per person)
3 tablespoons olive oil
salt and freshly ground black pepper
FILLING
smoked salmon, in small pieces
sprigs of dill

Preheat oven to 200C (400F/Gas 6). Boil the whole potatoes until just tender. Allow to cool for 10 minutes. Cut each boiled potato in half.

Scoop out middle of each potato using a teaspoon or melon baller. Place skins on a baking tray, cut side up. Drizzle skins with olive oil. Season with salt and pepper. Bake for 15-20 minutes until crispy and remove from oven.

Add about 2 teaspoons smoked salmon and sprinkle with pepper. Add a tiny sprig of fresh dill.

Other possible meat fillings are Bolognaise, curried chicken, turkey and cranberry sauce. Milk fillings could include guacamole, or ripe Brie, black grapes and toasted almonds. Parev fillings could include humous and red pepper, or garden pea and cumin purée. Serve hot or cold.

*Parev*

# – OLIVE & CHEESE PASTRY BALLS –

250g (9oz/2¼ cups) plain (all-purpose) flour
150g (5oz/⅔ cup) unsalted butter [margarine for
  Parev]
1 egg
160g (5½oz/1¼ cups) Gruyère cheese or strong
  Cheddar cheese, grated [3 tablespoons mixed fresh
  herbs e.g. basil, parsley, for Parev]
1 teaspoon dried cumin or dried coriander
400g (14oz) can black olives, pitted and drained

Preheat oven to 200C (400F/Gas 6). Make
cheese pastry by combining flour, butter,
egg, cheese and dried cumin or coriander in
your food processor.

Add 2-3 tablespoons cold water to bring
dough together into a ball. Flatten pastry
ball and wrap in clear film (plastic wrap).
Chill in the fridge for 30 minutes.

Roll pastry out quite thinly on a lightly
floured surface. Using a 5cm (2in) round
cutter, cut out circles of pastry. Place a black
olive in centre of each circle. Encase olive
in pastry and roll to form a small ball. Line a
baking sheet with baking parchment. Put all
the balls on the baking sheet and bake for
15-20 minutes until golden. Serve
immediately in a basket lined with salad or
cabbage leaves.

*Can be Parev*
*Makes about 35*

# -SUN-DRIED TOMATO TARTLETS-

300g (10oz/2½ cups) plain (all-purpose) flour
160g (5½oz/⅔ cup) unsalted butter
2 sun-dried tomatoes, roughly chopped
1 egg
FILLING
115g (4oz/½ cup) each garlic and herb cream cheese,
    and cottage cheese
1 egg
3 tablespoons finely chopped fresh herbs
salt and freshly ground black pepper
GARNISH
6 cherry tomatoes, thinly sliced
3 sun-dried tomatoes, thinly sliced
½ red and ½ yellow pepper (capsicum), very finely
    chopped
1 small bunch fresh basil

Preheat oven to 180C (350F/Gas 4). Place flour, butter, sun-dried tomatoes, and egg in a food processor, and process until a ball of dough is formed. Wrap in clear film (plastic wrap) and flatten. Refrigerate for 30 minutes. Put all filling ingredients in a food processor and process until combined.

Roll out pastry very thinly on a lightly floured surface. Using a 5cm (2in) round, plain cutter, make circles to fit into canapé trays. Line each canapé cup with a pastry circle easing it in gently. Fill each cup with 1 teaspoon of filling. Bake for 20 minutes. Remove from oven and garnish with cherry tomatoes, chopped sun-dried tomatoes, chopped pepper (capsicum) and torn basil leaves.

*Makes 35*

# — STILTON & SHERRY CROSTINI —

PATÉ
50g (2oz/½ cup) pine nuts
25g (1oz/2 tablespoons) butter
1 small red pepper (capsicum), finely chopped
1 small onion, finely chopped
50g (2oz/¼ cup) cream cheese
50g (2oz/¼ cup) dolcelatte or blue cheese
1 teaspoon Dijon mustard
85g (3oz/¾ cup) Stilton
1 tablespoon dry sherry
CROSTINI
1 loaf French bread
150ml (5fl oz/⅔ cup) olive oil

To make pâté, put pine nuts into a dry frying pan (skillet) and cook until golden brown. Set aside. Heat butter in same frying pan (skillet). Add red pepper (capsicum) and onion and sauté over a medium heat until onion is transparent. Transfer pepper (capsicum) and onion to a food processor and add cream cheese and dolcelatte, mustard, Stilton and sherry. Process until smooth. Reserve 15g (½oz) of pine nuts for garnish; add remaining pine nuts to pâté and pulse again. Use immediately or refrigerate until required.

To make crostini, preheat oven to 200C (400F/Gas 6). Slice French bread. Brush both sides of every slice with olive oil and place on a baking sheet. Bake for 10 minutes. Allow to cool before spreading with pâté. Cut each slice into three and garnish with roasted pine nuts. Serve topped with a sliver of red pepper (capsicum) and fresh thyme.

*Makes 35*

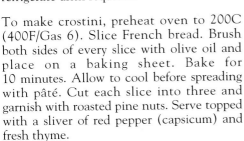

# —— CHICKEN FILO TARTLETS ——

TARTLETS
filo pastry sheets (total size needed at least 25 x
    45cm (10 x 18in))
2 tablespoons olive oil
2 egg yolks, beaten
FILLING
2 tablespoons sesame oil
1 boneless, skinless chicken breast, cut into very
    small pieces
1 tablespoon soy sauce
3 spring onions (scallions), finely chopped
1 clove garlic, crushed
1 teaspoon ground coriander
1 teaspoon honey
1 bunch coriander (cilantro) leaves, to garnish

To make the tartlet cases, preheat oven to
200C (400F/Gas 6). Using a 5cm (2in)
round cutter, cut filo into 45 circles. Mix
olive oil with beaten egg yolk. Brush each
circle with egg mixture and place it in an
oiled mini canapé tin (the circles should be
the same size as tin). Place 3 circle layers of
filo in each of 15 cups. Bake filo cases for
about 10 minutes until golden brown.

For the filling, heat sesame oil in a small
frying pan (skillet) or wok. Add all the
filling ingredients and stir fry for 5 minutes
until chicken is cooked. When you are
ready to serve, fill the warmed tartlet cases
with the hot chicken. Arrange on a serving
plate and garnish with coriander (cilantro)
leaves.

*Makes 15*

## —— APRICOT SAUSAGE PUFFS ——

225g (8oz) sausage meat or minced (ground) lamb
1 egg
15g (½oz) fresh sage, stalks removed
15g (½oz) fresh mint, stalks removed
50g (2oz/⅓ cup) dried apricots
375g (13oz) puff pastry, ready rolled if possible
salt and freshly ground black pepper
2 egg yolks, beaten

Preheat oven to 220C (425F/Gas 7). Put meat, egg, sage, mint, apricots and salt and pepper together in a food processor and process until combined.

If not ready rolled, roll out pastry into 12 x 35cm (4½ x 14in) rectangle on a lightly floured surface; trim. Spread meat filling down length, over approximately half width, leaving 1cm (½in) border round edge. Fold pastry over to cover and pinch edges tightly together giving a wavy seal.

Line a baking sheet with baking parchment. Glaze pastry with the beaten egg yolk. Cut filled pastry into approximately 18 slices and arrange on prepared baking sheet. Bake for 15-20 minutes until golden brown and crispy. These can be served hot or cold, or frozen when cooled.

*Makes 18*

# MEXICAN CORN CUPS

**CORN CUPS**
170g (6oz/¾ cup) butter, softened
85g (3oz) cream cheese
225g (8oz/2 cups) plain (all-purpose) flour
115g (4oz/1 cup) fine polenta
1 tablespoon chopped fresh coriander (cilantro)
pinch of cayenne pepper
pinch of salt
**FILLING**
guacamole, chilli beans, tomato salsa, or refried beans

To make the corn cups, preheat the oven to 180C (350F/Gas 4). Cream together butter and cream cheese.

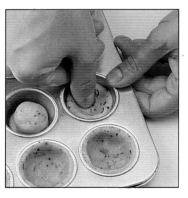

Gradually add flour, polenta, coriander (cilantro), cayenne, 1 tablespoon cold water and the salt to form a soft dough. Knead gently. Roll a walnut-sized piece of dough into a ball. Press the ball down into small canapé tins. Ease dough up the sides to form a little cup. Bake for 20 minutes or until golden.

Fill each cup with about 1 teaspoon of your chosen filling and serve immediately.

*Makes 50*

# SPINACH CHOUX BITES

**CHOUX PASTRY**
85g (3oz) butter
115g (4oz/½ cup) plain (all-purpose) flour
3 eggs, beaten
115g (4oz) mozzarella cheese, finely diced
10 basil leaves, roughly torn
salt and freshly ground black pepper
**FILLING**
225g (8oz) spinach, cooked, chopped and drained
  well
115g (4oz/½ cup) soft garlic cream cheese
1 large bunch basil, finely torn
2 tablespoons grated Parmesan cheese (optional)

To make choux pastry, preheat oven to 200C (400F/Gas 6). Pour 200ml (7fl oz) cold water into a medium-sized saucepan. Add butter and melt over a low heat. Increase heat and bring to a rolling boil. Remove from heat and immediately add all the flour. Beat to a smooth paste. Return to a low heat to dry a little, then cool until tepid. Add eggs gradually, beating well between each addition. Add mozzarella, torn basil leaves and salt and pepper.

Place heaped spoonfuls of dough on to a baking sheet lined with damp baking parchment, leaving a space between each. Bake for 15 minutes until puffed and golden. Cool. For filling, blend spinach, cream cheese and basil together until smooth. Season well. Make a slit in each choux bite. Fill each bite with 1 teaspoon filling. Place bites back on to lined baking sheet. Sprinkle with Parmesan cheese, if using. Reheat in oven for 3-5 minutes.

*Makes about 20*

# — CRANBERRY & TURKEY BITES —

450g (1lb) minced (ground) raw turkey
2 tablespoons cranberry jelly
50g (2oz/½ cup) fine matzoh meal
1 egg, beaten
20g (¾oz) fresh mint
salt and freshly ground black pepper
20g (¾oz) dried cranberries
25g (1oz/¼ cup) chopped pecan nuts
2 litres (70fl oz/9 cups) chicken stock
1 large savoy cabbage, inner core removed but
  keeping the outer leaves
DIPPING SAUCE
200g (7oz/⅔ cup) jellied cranberry sauce
3 tablespoons Kiddush wine

Mix turkey, cranberry jelly, matzoh meal, egg, mint and salt and pepper in a food processor. Carefully add cranberries and pecan nuts and pulse quickly to combine but still maintain some texture. Make into little ball shapes (bite-size portions.) Heat chicken stock until it simmers and add turkey bites; simmer for about 10 minutes. Meanwhile, make dipping sauce by mixing both the ingredients together in a small saucepan. Simmer for 5 minutes until well combined.

Drain the turkey bites. To serve, place the turkey bites inside the carved out savoy cabbage and serve immediately with the dipping sauce in a separate small dish.

*Pesach friendly*
*Makes 40*

# —— TRIO OF SALMON RISOTTO ——

2 tablespoons olive oil
50g (2oz/¼ cup) butter
2 onions, finely chopped
150ml (5fl oz/⅔ cup) white wine
1.1 litres (40fl oz/5 cups) vegetable stock
225g (8oz/1 cup) Arborio or Carnoli rice
225g (8oz) fresh salmon, skinned and cubed
6 tablespoons snipped fresh chives
115g (4oz) smoked salmon, cut into bite-size pieces
115g (4oz) gravad lax, cut into bite-size pieces
3 tablespoons Parmesan (optional)
salt and freshly ground black pepper

Heat olive oil and butter in a deep frying pan (skillet), and fry onions until softened.

Mix white wine with vegetable stock and heat in a separate saucepan until it is very hot. Add rice to onions and continue to fry until rice is translucent, about 3 minutes. Turn heat to a low simmer whilst you add one ladle of hot stock at a time to rice. Continue gradually adding hot stock until rice becomes just tender and most of stock has been absorbed. Stir frequently to prevent rice from sticking.

Add fresh salmon and half the chives with last ladle of stock, mix well and continue to cook until salmon is cooked. Remove from heat and add smoked salmon, gravad lax, Parmesan cheese, if using, and salt and pepper. Garnish with remaining snipped chives, and serve immediately, sprinkled with extra Parmesan shavings.

*Can be Parev*
*Serves 8-10 as a starter; 4-6 as a main course*

# - CHICKEN LIVER CAESAR SALAD -

575g (1¼lb) chicken livers
6 slices brown or white bread, crusts removed and
    cubed
3 tablespoons olive oil
salt and freshly ground black pepper
2 tablespoons grated soya Parmesan (optional)
175g (6oz) baby leeks
115g (4oz) asparagus tips
4 Little Gem lettuces
4 tablespoons dried cranberries
4 tablespoons capers, rinsed
1 large egg, beaten
4 tablespoons plain (all-purpose) flour
3 tablespoons vegetable oil
4 tablespoons red wine

Kosher chicken livers; wash livers. Place on
foil in a grill (broiler) pan. Sprinkle with
cooking salt. Grill (broil) until livers change
colour. Turn over and grill (broil) on other
side. Rinse off any excess salt. (Discard foil
after use as this is not Kosher.) Wash and
drain chicken livers.

Preheat the oven to 200C (400F/Gas 6).
Place bread cubes on a baking sheet lined
with baking parchment. Drizzle with olive
oil. Season with salt and pepper and
sprinkle with soya cheese, if using. Bake for
10 minutes. Remove from oven and cool on
baking sheet. Set aside.

Cut baby leeks lengthways into four. Bring a saucepan of water to a boil and cook leeks and asparagus until al dente. Refresh in cold water to maintain colour and crispness. Drain and set aside.

Split lettuces and cut centre cores into 4 segments. Decorate plate with a circular pattern of lettuce, asparagus and leeks. Scatter with dried cranberries and capers.

Coat chicken livers in beaten egg and seasoned flour. Heat vegetable oil in a large frying pan (skillet) until very hot. Add chicken livers and stir carefully for 2-3 minutes. Add red wine and cook for another 2 minutes. Arrange chicken livers on lettuce leaves, asparagus and leeks, and scatter with croutons.

*Serves 4*

# SMOKED TROUT SOUFFLÉ

85g (3oz/⅓ cup) butter, for greasing
50g (2oz/1 cup) fresh breadcrumbs [or medium matzoh meal for Pesach]
85g (3oz/⅓ cup) butter
50g (2oz/½ cup) plain (all-purpose) flour [potato flour for Pesach]
300ml (10fl oz/1¼ cups) milk
115g (4oz) smoked trout fillets, skinned
2 tablespoons double (heavy) cream or cream cheese
5 egg yolks, beaten
50g (2oz) fresh dill
pinch of nutmeg
salt and freshly ground black pepper
6 egg whites

Grease sides and base of 8 ramekins with butter. Coat inside with breadcrumbs, shaking out any excess. Make a collar out of baking parchment and secure around the outside of each ramekin with string. Follow same instructions to prepare a 23cm (9in) soufflé dish. Preheat oven to 200C (400F/Gas 6). Make a white sauce by melting the butter in a small saucepan. Add flour and cook for 1 minute over a low heat. Slowly add milk, stirring continuously until thickened. Remove from heat and set aside.

Mash trout with cream or cream cheese. Stir egg yolks, fish and dill into white sauce. Add nutmeg, a little salt, and plenty of pepper. Beat egg whites until soft peaks form. Fold 1 tablespoon of beaten egg white into fish mixture, using a metal spoon in a figure of eight movement. Add remaining egg whites, folding in lightly. Pour mixture into prepared ramekins or soufflé dish. Bake ramekins for 25 minutes or 45 minutes for the single dish. Serve immediately.

*Pesach friendly - Serves 8*

# - PENNE & PARMESAN FRITTATA -

200g (7oz) dried penne (pasta)
2 tablespoons olive oil
2 onions, finely chopped
½ red pepper (capsicum), finely chopped
100g (3½oz) cherry tomatoes, skinned and halved
6 eggs
115g (4 oz/1 cup) freshly grated Parmesan cheese
115ml (4fl oz/½ cup) milk
3 tablespoons coarsely chopped fresh herbs e.g.
   thyme, chives, basil, sage
salt and freshly ground black pepper
GARNISH
8 slices freshly shaved Parmesan cheese
8 sprigs thyme

Preheat the oven to 190C (375F/Gas 5).
Cook the penne in salted boiling water until
al dente. Meanwhile, heat the olive oil in a
large frying pan (skillet). Fry onions and
pepper (capsicum) over a medium heat until
softened. Add tomatoes. Cook for a further
5 minutes. Leave to cool. Combine eggs,
cheese, milk and herbs in a large bowl and
whisk well. Stir in tomato mixture and pasta
and season to taste.

Line a 23cm (9in) spring-form baking tin
with baking parchment and grease with a
little oil. Spoon in the mixture. Bake for
40 minutes or until set. To serve, turn the
frittata out on to a serving platter; remove
the baking parchment. Cut into wedges and
serve warm. Garnish with large shavings of
Parmesan on top and scatter with thyme
and black pepper.

*Serves 6*

# —— GOAT'S CHEESE TERRINE ——

2 each large red and yellow peppers (capsicums),
   quartered
2 tablespoons olive oil
300g (10oz) Desirée potatoes, thinly sliced
15g (½ oz/1 tablespoon) butter
1 leek, finely chopped
2 eggs
300ml (10fl oz/1¼ cups) soured (sour) cream
85g (3oz/⅓ cup) soft goat's cheese [or similar for
   Pesach]
50g (2oz) fresh basil, torn
salt and freshly ground black pepper

Grease and line a 900g (2lb) loaf tin (pan)
with baking parchment.

Preheat the oven to 180C (350F/Gas 4).
Brush peppers (capsicums) with olive oil
and grill (broil) skin side up until they start
to blister. Put peppers (capsicums) into a
bowl and cover with clear film (plastic
wrap); when cool remove skin. Cook
potatoes in boiling salted water until just
tender. Drain and leave to cool. Melt butter
in a small frying pan (skillet) and sauté leek
until softened. Leave to cool. Combine eggs,
soured (sour) cream and goat's cheese and
mix until smooth. Add leeks, basil, salt and
pepper and mix.

Spoon one third of egg mixture into loaf tin
(pan). Layer with half potato, the red pepper
(capsicum) and half remaining egg mixture.
Repeat with yellow pepper (capsicum),
potato and remaining egg mixture. Cover
tightly with greased foil and place in a
roasting tin (pan). Pour in enough hot water
to come half-way up side of loaf tin (a bain
marie). Bake for 70 minutes. Uncover and
cook for a further 30 minutes. Remove from
bain marie and let stand for 1 hour. Turn
out, cut into slices and serve warm or cold.

*Pesach friendly - Serves 6-8*

# — PICKLED HERRING COCKTAIL —

3 pickled herrings, skinned
6 slices smoked salmon
1 red apple, cut into quarters
zest and juice of 1 lemon
1 mixed bag salad leaves including rocket (arugula)
  and watercress, roughly chopped
½ green cucumber, roughly chopped
150ml (5fl oz/⅔ cup) soured (sour) cream
6 sprigs dill, stalks removed
freshly ground black pepper
GARNISH
6 slices rye bread
butter, for spreading
2 lemons, cut into wedges

Slice pickled herrings in half lengthwise.
Lay a slice of smoked salmon on a board.
Place a slice of pickled herring on top of the
salmon. Roll lengthways to form a long
'sausage roll'. Using a sharp knife slice into
1cm (½in) thick pinwheel circles. Repeat
this with remaining 5 herring slices and
5 salmon slices. Chop apple into small
cubes. Toss cubes in lemon juice and discard
excess juice.

In a bowl, mix chopped salad leaves with
the herring pinwheels, apple and chopped
cucumber. In a separate dish, combine
soured (sour) cream with dill, lemon zest
and pepper. Mix soured (sour) cream
mixture into salad ingredients and spoon
equally into 6 small bowls. Grind some more
black pepper on top. To serve, spread rye
bread with butter. Cut into triangles and
serve to the side of the cocktail, with the
lemon wedges. Serve immediately.

*Serves 6*

# –BRIOCHE & WILD MUSHROOMS–

3 tablespoons olive oil
1 red onion, finely chopped
4 cloves garlic, crushed
900g (2lb) wild mushrooms e.g. a mixture of brown
  cap, oyster, shiitake, button, chanterelles, cèpes,
  girolles, roughly chopped
3 tablespoons red wine
300ml (10fl oz/1¼ cups) double (heavy) cream
2 tablespoons white or black truffle oil (optional)
salt and freshly ground black pepper
10 brioche
1 bunch parsley, finely chopped, to garnish

Heat the oil in a large frying pan (skillet).
Fry the red onion and garlic until softened.

Add mushrooms and continue to fry until
softened. Add red wine, cream and truffle
oil (if using). Increase heat to reduce some
excess liquid and to cook off raw alcohol
taste. Season well with salt and pepper.

Preheat the oven to 180C (350F/Gas 4).
Remove the tops from each brioche. Scoop
out the inside of the 'body' of each brioche.
Place the 'bodies' and tops on a baking
sheet. Warm in the oven for 5 minutes.
Spoon hot mushroom mixture into each
brioche. Replace the tops and garnish with
chopped parsley; serve immediately on
warmed plates.

*Makes 10*

# STUFFED SUGAR SNAPS

130g (4½oz) sugar snaps
115g (4oz/½ cup) cream cheese
2 tablespoons snipped chives
2 tablespoons finely chopped parsley
salt and freshly ground black pepper
115g (4oz) smoked salmon pâté

Using a small sharp knife, open each sugar snap by tracing along curved edge with the point.

Bring a small saucepan of water to the boil and immerse the sugar snaps for 1 minute to blanch. Remove immediately, drain, refresh under cold water and dry.

Mix cream cheese, herbs, salt and pepper together. Pipe cheese mixture and salmon pâté separately into sugar snaps, using a small pointed or serrated nozzle (tube). Gently press ends of sugar snaps together. Serve arranged alternately on a plate.

*Makes about 25*

# – HADDOCK & ORANGE TERRINE –

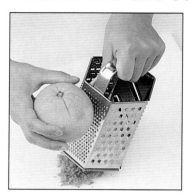

3 oranges, plus 2 tablespoons orange juice
225g (8oz) haddock or cod, skinned, boned and
  cubed
4 tablespoons chopped fresh dill
salt and freshly ground black pepper
2 egg whites
150ml (5fl oz/⅔ cup) whipping (heavy) cream [or
  Parev cream]
225g (8oz) smoked salmon
2 heads chicory, leaves separated
3 tablespoons walnut oil
1 tablespoon raspberry vinegar
1 tablespoon caster (superfine) sugar

Grate 1 tablespoon orange rind (zest).

Preheat the oven to 180C (350F/Gas 4).
Place orange rind (zest) in a food processor
with haddock, 2 tablespoons orange juice,
half the dill and pepper. Process until
smooth. Cover and chill in freezer for
10 minutes. Lightly oil a 900g terrine
(2lb loaf tin) and line base with baking
parchment. Put haddock in processor again
and, with machine running, add egg whites
through feed tube. Add cream and process
very briefly. Pulse in salmon. Carefully fill
terrine with mixture, packing it down well.
Cover terrine with baking parchment.

Stand terrine in a roasting tin (pan) and add
hot water to come halfway up side of terrine
(a bain marie). Bake for 35-40 minutes or
until firm. Run a knife around terrine and
unmould on to a board. Peel and segment
oranges, removing pith and membrane. Toss
oranges, chicory and remaining dill. Mix oil,
vinegar, sugar and seasoning and toss with
salad. Cut terrine into slices, arrange on
plates and garnish with dill. Serve with salad.

*Can be Parev. Pesach friendly (terrine only)*
*Serves 6*

# SPICY MUSHROOM SOUP

115g (4oz) dried mushrooms
2 lemon grass stalks
1 litre (35fl oz/4½ cups) vegetable stock
2 spring onions (scallions), thinly sliced
2 shallots, thinly sliced
450g (1lb) mushrooms e.g. black cap, oyster, wild
   mushrooms, sliced
4 large tomatoes, skinned, deseeded and chopped
2 small red chillies, deseeded and sliced
2.5cm (1in) fresh root ginger, finely chopped
2 cloves garlic, crushed
4 tablespoons lemon juice
1 teaspoon Chinese five-spice powder
1 tablespoon light soy sauce
coriander (cilantro) leaves, to garnish

Cover dried mushrooms in boiling water
and soak for 10 minutes. Cut lemon grass
into 2.5cm (1in) lengths. In a large
saucepan heat stock with lemon grass,
spring onions (scallions) and shallots. Bring
to the boil and simmer for 2 minutes. Add
all mushrooms, including soaking water.
Cover and simmer for 5 minutes.

Stir in tomatoes, chillies, ginger, garlic,
lemon juice, Chinese five-spice and soy
sauce. Simmer for 10 minutes. Remove from
heat. Remove and discard lemon grass
pieces. Garnish with coriander (cilantro)
leaves.

*Can be Parev. Pesach friendly*
*Serves 6*

# SOUPE DE POISSON

6-10 bones and head from seabass, red mullet or
   bream (available from your fishmonger)
1 large leek, chopped
2 red onions, chopped
2 carrots, chopped
6 cloves garlic
1 bunch fresh thyme
150ml (5fl oz/⅔ cup) red wine
1 teaspoon paprika
salt and freshly ground black pepper
2 litres (70fl oz/9 cups) well-flavoured vegetable stock

Preheat the oven to 200C (400F/Gas 6).
Place all the ingredients except the stock in
a roasting tin (pan), adding a little water.

Roast vegetables for 30 minutes.
Meanwhile, in a large pan, bring stock to a
simmer. Remove roasting tin (pan) from
oven and add contents to hot stock.
Liquidize stock and solids (in batches if
necessary), until smooth.

Pass each batch through a fine sieve into a
large, clean pan. Liquidize the contents of
the sieve to yield more soup. Strain this
soup through a fine sieve and add to pan.
Continue until all the stock and solids have
been processed. Heat soup, stirring
occasionally. Serve in individual warmed
bowls with a slice of lightly toasted French
bread, topped with freshly grated Gruyère
cheese, floating on top.

*Serves 10-12*

# —GINGER SPICED PARSNIP SOUP—

3 tablespoons olive oil
225g (8oz) carrots, chopped
225g (8oz) parsnips, chopped
2 small onions or 4 spring onions (scallions),
  chopped
2 leeks or 2 sticks celery, chopped
5cm (2in) fresh root ginger, grated
1.4 litres (50fl oz/6¼ cups) vegetable stock
175g (6oz/1 cup) red split lentils
salt and freshly ground black pepper
200ml (7fl oz/scant 1 cup) soured (sour) cream,
  Greek-style yogurt or crème fraîche [omit for Parev]
1 teaspoon hot curry paste
chopped celery leaves, fresh parsley or fresh
  coriander (cilantro), to garnish

Heat olive oil in a large saucepan and sauté
carrots, parsnips, onions, leeks or celery and
ginger until soft. Add vegetable stock and
lentils. Simmer for 20-25 minutes until
vegetables and lentils are tender. Season to
taste with salt and pepper.

In a bowl, mix soured (sour) cream or
Greek-style yogurt or crème fraîche with
curry paste. To serve, ladle the soup out into
warmed deep bowls and place a spoonful of
creamed curry paste on top. Garnish with
celery leaves, coriander (cilantro) or parsley.
Serve immediately with chunks of ciabatta
or French bread.

*Can be Parev*
*Serves 6*

# SUMMER PEA SOUP

2 tablespoons vegetable oil
8 spring onions (scallions), sliced
850ml (30fl oz/3¾ cups) vegetable stock
1kg (2lb) fresh peas in the pod, podded or
   450g (1lb) frozen petits pois
2 tablespoons chopped fresh mint
½ green lettuce, shredded
115g (4oz) mange-tout (snow peas), chopped
salt and freshly ground black pepper
mint sprigs, to garnish

Heat vegetable oil in a large deep saucepan and gently fry spring onions (scallions) until softened.

Add the stock and stir in the peas and chopped mint. Bring to the boil and simmer for 10 minutes (5 minutes for frozen peas). Add the lettuce, chopped mange-tout (snow peas) and seasoning. Simmer again for 5 minutes.

Purée half the soup in a blender or food processor. Return purée to saucepan and mix well. Serve piping hot, garnished with mint sprigs.

*Can be Parev*
*Serves 4-6*

# —— CARROT & CELERIAC SOUP ——

3 tablespoons olive oil
3 shallots, finely chopped
4 cloves garlic, finely chopped
1 celeriac (celery root), grated or shredded
6 carrots, grated or shredded
1.7 litres (60fl oz/7½ cups) vegetable or chicken
  stock
225g (8oz) baby spinach, stalks removed and chopped
3 slices thick cut smoked turkey, cut into matchsticks

Heat the olive oil in a large saucepan. Add
the shallots and garlic and lightly fry until
transluscent but not coloured.

Add the grated celeriac (celery root), and
carrots and the stock. Simmer for 15-20
minutes.

Add the chopped baby spinach and turkey.
Cook for a further 5 minutes. Serve at once
or allow to cool before refrigerating or
freezing.

*Pesach friendly*
*Serves 6*

# — SHERRY BLACK BEAN SOUP —

450g (1lb) black beans, soaked overnight
2 tablespoons olive oil
2 large onions, finely chopped
8 cloves garlic, finely chopped
2 litres (70fl oz/9 cups) chicken or vegetable stock
2 tablespoons cumin seeds
3 tablespoons chopped fresh oregano
3 bay leaves, dried or fresh
pinch of cayenne pepper
4 tablespoons chopped fresh parsley
1 red pepper (capsicum) finely chopped
200ml (7fl oz/scant 1 cup) dry sherry
juice of 2 lemons
1 tablespoon soft brown sugar
salt and freshly ground black pepper

Drain beans, cover with fresh water, bring to the boil and continue to boil rapidly for 10 minutes. Drain and rinse. Heat olive oil in a large saucepan and sauté onions and garlic until softened but not coloured.

Add beans, stock, cumin seeds, oregano, bay leaves, cayenne and 2 tablespoons of parsley. Bring to the boil and cover. Reduce heat and simmer for 2 hours. Stir in red pepper (capsicum), sherry, lemon juice, remaining chopped parsley and brown sugar. Simmer for a further 10 minutes. Season to taste. Remove and discard bay leaves and serve hot in warmed bowls.

*Can be Parev*
*Serves 12*

# SQUASH & COD CHOWDER

900g (2lb) butternut squash, peeled and cut into
  2.5cm (1in) cubes
4 tablespoons olive oil
3 cloves garlic, finely chopped
salt and freshly ground black pepper
1 large onion, finely chopped
1.4 litres (50fl oz/6¼ cups) vegetable stock
225g (8oz) smoked cod, skinned and cubed
2 x 350g (12oz) cans sweetcorn
coriander (cilantro) leaves, to garnish

Preheat oven to 200C (400F/Gas 6). Place
squash in a roasting tin (pan). Drizzle with
2 tablespoons olive oil and sprinkle with
chopped garlic. Season with salt and pepper.

Roast for 20 minutes. In a large saucepan,
sauté onion in remaining 2 tablespoons of
olive oil until softened but not coloured.
Bring the vegetable stock to simmering
point and add to the pan with the onion;
add the cod and sweetcorn. Bring to the
boil.

Add the roasted butternut squash and
simmer for 15 minutes. Ladle the soup into
warmed bowls and garnish with coriander
(cilantro) leaves.

**Variations:** Use pumpkin when in season.
Add broad (fava) beans and a selection of
wild mushrooms if you like. Use smoked
haddock instead of cod if you prefer.

*Parev*
*Serves 6*

# — SQUASH & WHITE BEAN SOUP —

2 tablespoons olive oil
450g (1lb) butternut squash, peeled and cubed
2 onions, finely chopped
2 carrots, finely chopped
175g (6oz) baby leeks, thinly sliced
3 cloves garlic, crushed
2 litres (70fl oz/9 cups) vegetable stock
1 x 400g (14oz) can cannellini beans, drained and
   rinsed
2 tablespoons chopped flat-leaf parsley
2 tablespoons chopped basil
salt and freshly ground black pepper
GARLIC CROUTONS
6 slices day-old bread, crusts removed
2 cloves garlic, crushed
2 tablespoons extra virgin olive oil

Heat olive oil in a large saucepan. Sauté butternut squash, onions, carrots, leeks and garlic. Cook for 10 minutes over a low heat. Add the stock. Bring to the boil. Simmer for 15-20 minutes. Add beans and herbs and season to taste.

To make the garlic croutons, preheat the oven to 200C (400F/Gas 6). Cut bread into 1cm (½in) cubes and scatter on baking sheet. Mix crushed garlic with olive oil and drizzle over bread cubes. Season with salt and pepper. Bake for 10 minutes, taking care they do not burn. Remove from the oven. Serve soup hot, sprinkled with croutons.

**Variation:** Pumpkin can be used in place of butternut squash.

# — SUN-DRIED TOMATO ROLLS —

450g (1lb/4 cups) white strong (bread) flour
2 teaspoons salt
7g (¼oz/1 sachet) dried yeast
2 tablespoons extra virgin olive oil
2 tablespoons sun-dried tomatoes, finely chopped and
   soaked in olive oil
1-2 egg yolks, for glazing
extra virgin olive oil, for greasing bowl

Sift flour and salt into a large bowl. Add yeast, olive oil, sun-dried tomatoes and 425ml (15fl oz/scant 2 cups) warm water. Mix well until a firm dough has formed.

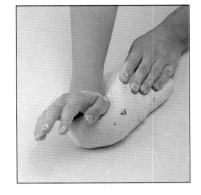

Place the dough in an oiled bowl, cover and leave to rise for about 1½ hours in a warm place. Preheat oven to 230C (450F/Gas 8). Knock back dough and divide dough into 12 and then divide each into 3 equal pieces. Knead and roll out each piece to a thin 'sausage'. Line up 3 thin 'sausages' so that they cross over at the centre and start to plait (braid), beginning at centre and working towards you. Turn dough around and complete other side. Press ends together and tuck under neatly.

Place rolls on a baking sheet lined with baking parchment and glaze with egg yolk. Bake for 10 minutes, reduce the heat to 200C (400F/Gas 6) and bake rolls for 20-25 minutes until golden brown. Remove from oven and place on a wire rack.

**Variation:** Add 2 tablespoons chopped fresh basil and/or 50g (2oz) black olives into the basic dough.

*Parev - Makes 12 rolls*

# — ROSEMARY CIABATTA ROLLS —

7g (¼oz/1 sachet) dried yeast
2 teaspoons salt
750g (1lb 10oz/6½ cups) white strong (bread) flour
1 tablespoon maple syrup or clear honey
150ml (5fl oz/⅔ cup) extra virgin olive oil
25g (1oz) fresh rosemary, finely chopped
olive oil, for drizzling
sea salt, for sprinkling

Mix together the yeast, salt and flour. Add maple syrup or honey, oil and half the chopped rosemary until well combined. The mixture should become soft and shiny.

Mix together slowly using a dough hook if available. Gradually add 425ml (15fl oz/ scant 2 cups) warm water until combined (you may not need to use all the water). Transfer into an oiled bowl, cover and leave to rise in a warm place for 1½ hours or until doubled in size.

Preheat oven to 220C (425F/Gas 7). Knock back dough. Divide into 15 pieces. Knead and then flatten each roll. Place on a baking sheet lined with baking parchment. Make thumb indentations and then drizzle with olive oil, sprinkle with sea salt and remaining chopped rosemary leaves. Leave to prove for 10 minutes. Bake rolls on the middle shelf for 20 minutes or until golden brown. Cool on a wire rack.

*Parev*
*Makes 15 rolls*

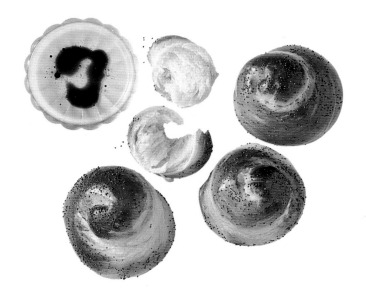

# — BABY CHALLAH-STYLE ROLLS —

7g (¼oz/1 sachet) dried yeast
2 teaspoons salt
575g (1¼lb) white strong (bread) flour
2 tablespoons clear honey
85ml (3fl oz/⅓ cup) olive oil
2 eggs, beaten
2 egg yolks, for glazing
4 teaspoons poppy seeds, to decorate
100ml (3⅓fl oz/scant ½ cup) extra virgin olive oil
1 tablespoons balsamic vinegar

Mix together yeast, salt and 200ml (7fl oz/
scant 1 cup) warm water. Add this to the
flour. Mix together slowly either by hand or
in a mixer using a dough hook.

Add honey, olive oil and egg. Continue to
knead mixture until smooth and shiny. You
may need a little extra warm water. Transfer
to an oiled bowl, cover and leave to rise for
2 hours in a warm place. Knock back dough.
Divide dough into 100g (4oz) portions and
roll each portion into a long rope. Hold one
end and coil rope of dough around into a
spiral shape, so that centre of spiral rises up
slightly. Tuck the outside end underneath
to make a neat finish.

Line a baking sheet with baking parchment.
Place rolls on sheet. Preheat oven to 200C
(400F/Gas 6). Leave to prove for
20 minutes. Glaze with egg glaze and
sprinkle with poppy seeds. Bake for
25 minutes or until golden brown and
sounding hollow when tapped on base. Cool
on a wire rack. Mix extra virgin olive oil
and balsamic vinegar in a little glass bowl
and serve for dipping.

*Makes 10*

# - CRUSTY CUMIN & CORN BREAD -

130g (4½oz) ground polenta
2 tablespoons olive oil
1 tablespoon cumin seeds, dry roasted
15g (½oz) sea salt
15g (½oz/2 sachets) dried yeast
200g (7oz) cooked corn kernels, fresh frozen or
    canned
600g (1lb 5oz) white strong (bread) flour
2 tablespoons polenta, plus extra for dusting

Bring 425ml (15fl oz/scant 2 cups) water to
boil in a saucepan. Add polenta in a steady
stream stirring constantly with a whisk.

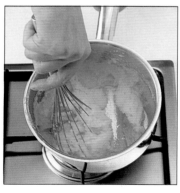

Continue to stir over a medium heat for 30-
60 seconds until polenta forms a mass and
leaves side of pan. Remove from heat, stir in
olive oil, cumin seeds and salt. Leave to
cool.

In a large mixing bowl, dissolve yeast in
2½ teaspoons warm water. Add polenta
mixture and corn and beat with an electric
mixer using a dough hook until well
combined. Gradually add strong (bread)
flour and mix for 10 minutes until dough is
smooth and elastic.

Flour your hands, and shape dough into a ball. Place in an oiled bowl, cover with clear film (plastic wrap) and leave to rise in a warm place for about 1½ hours until doubled in size.

Line a baking sheet with baking parchment and sprinkle extra polenta over. Knock back and cut dough in half. Preheat the oven to 220C (425F/Gas 7). Sprinkle flour on to a flat surface and knead dough into 2 round loaves about 15-18cm (6-7in) in diameter. Cover with oiled clear film (plastic wrap) and leave to rise again for 40 minutes on prepared baking sheet.

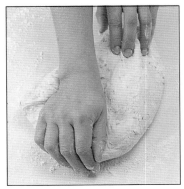

Remove clear film (plastic wrap). Make 3 slits in top of dough with a sharp knife. Glaze loaf with egg yolk. Place in oven with a roasting tin (pan) underneath which has been half filled with boiling water. (This gives off steam during cooking and makes the bread crisp.) Bake bread on middle shelf for 50-55 minutes or until golden brown. The bread is cooked when it sounds hollow when tapped on base. Leave to cool on a wire rack.

*Can be Parev - Makes 2 loaves*

# ──── WALNUT FRUIT BREAD ────

15g (½oz/2 sachets) dried yeast
50ml (2fl oz/¼ cup) olive oil
50ml (2fl oz/¼ cup) walnut oil
1kg (2¼lb/9 cups) plain strong (bread) flour
25g (1oz/6 teaspoons) salt
85g (3oz/¾ cup) chopped walnuts
50g (2oz/½ cup) dried apricots, chopped
50g (2oz/⅓ cup) raisins
2 egg yolks, for glazing

Place the yeast, both oils, flour and salt into a mixing bowl. Mix well. Add walnuts, apricots, raisins and 550ml (20fl oz/2½ cups) warm water.

Knead by hand for 10 minutes or 2 minutes using a mixer. Place in an oiled bowl, cover with clear film (plastic wrap) and leave to rise in a warm place for 45 minutes or until doubled in size. Preheat oven to 220C (425F/Gas 7). Knock back and then divide in 6 pieces for mini-loaves or 12 pieces for rolls. Shape as desired and place on a baking sheet lined with baking parchment.

Glaze with egg yolk and leave to prove for 10 minutes Bake on the middle shelf for 15-20 minutes for rolls or 30 minutes for mini-loaves until golden brown. Remove from oven and cool on a wire rack.

*Parev*
*Makes 6 mini-loaves or 12 rolls*

# MUSHROOM-STUFFED TOMATOES

2 tablespoons olive oil
175g (6oz) chestnut mushrooms (or similar),
  coarsely chopped
1 green and 1 yellow courgette (zucchini) (or
  2 green), grated
4 garlic cloves, crushed
4cm (1½in) fresh root ginger, grated
115g (4oz/2 cups) breadcrumbs
4 tablespoons ground almonds
50g (2oz/½ cup) pine nuts
salt and freshly ground black pepper
115g (4oz/½ cup) soft goat's cheese
4 beef tomatoes
GARNISH
1 bag mixed salad leaves
extra virgin olive oil, for drizzling

Preheat the oven to 200C (400F/Gas 6).
Heat olive oil in a large saucepan. Sauté
mushrooms, grated courgette (zucchini),
garlic, and ginger for 3 minutes. Drain away
any excess liquid. Add breadcrumbs, ground
almonds and pine nuts. Season well with
salt and pepper. Keeping saucepan on the
heat, stir in goat's cheese so it melts into the
mixture. Set aside.

Slice tops off tomatoes. Scoop out cores and
seeds and spoon in filling. Place tomato 'lid'
on top. Bake for 30 minutes. To serve, sit
each tomato on a bed of mixed salad leaves.
Drizzle with extra virgin olive oil and season
with black pepper.

*Serves 4 as a starter; 2 as a main course*

# ——— COD WITH SQUASH PURÉE ———

4 tablespoons extra virgin olive oil
2 cloves garlic, chopped
700g (1½lb) butternut squash, chopped
2 tablespoons chopped fresh sage
salt and freshly ground black pepper
50g (2oz/½ cup) unsalted butter or margarine
4 cod fillets, about 150g (5oz) each
juice of ½ lemon
1 tablespoon balsamic vinegar
2 tablespoons capers, rinsed [omit for Pesach]
2 tomatoes, skinned, deseeded and diced
1 tablespoon finely chopped fresh flat-leaf parsley
4 sprigs parsley, to garnish

Heat half the olive oil in a heavy saucepan
and sauté garlic for 3 minutes until golden.

Add squash and sage and stir-fry for 1-2
minutes. Add 4 tablespoons of water and
simmer gently for 30 minutes until squash is
cooked. Mash squash until very smooth,
beating in a little extra olive oil and salt and
pepper. Cover and keep warm. Preheat oven
to 190C (375F/Gas 5). Melt butter or
margarine and remaining olive oil in a
frying pan (skillet) until golden brown and
foaming.

Add cod, skin side down, and fry for 2-3
minutes, until crisp and browned. Turn
fillets over and fry for a further 2-3 minutes.
Transfer to an ovenproof dish. Season and
sprinkle with lemon juice, balsamic vinegar,
capers (if using), tomatoes and chopped
parsley. Cover and bake in the oven for
5 minutes. Spoon squash on to 4 plates.
Place a fillet on top of each mound with a
little cooking juices. Garnish with parsley
and serve.

*Can be Parev. Pesach friendly - Serves 4*

# ————'BEST EVER' FISH PIE————

900g (2lb) fish e.g. fresh and smoked cod, fresh and
  smoked haddock, skinned and cubed
300ml (10fl oz/1¼ cups) milk
225g (8oz) peas [mushrooms for Pesach]
250g (9oz) unsalted butter
3 onions, finely sliced
1 tablespoon ground cumin
2 tablespoons ground coriander
2 tablespoons mild curry powder [omit for Pesach]
50g (2oz/½ cup) plain (all-purpose) flour
300ml (10fl oz/1¼ cups) plus 2 tablespoons double
  (heavy) cream
salt and freshly ground black pepper
3 hard-boiled eggs, chopped
3 tablespoons chopped fresh parsley
6-8 large potatoes, cut into quarters

Preheat oven to 200C (400F/Gas 6). Place
fish in a large ovenproof dish. Pour milk
over and cover. Bake for 20 minutes. Drain
milk into a jug and make up to original
quantity if necessary. Transfer fish to a deep
oven-to-table serving dish. Cook peas (or
mushrooms). Melt 150g (5oz) butter in a
large saucepan and fry onions until softened
but not coloured. Add cumin, coriander and
curry powder, if using, and cook for
1 minute. Add flour. Cook for 1 minute.
Slowly add milk and 300ml (10fl oz/
1¼ cups) cream.

Stir sauce until a thin custard consistency.
Season well with salt and pepper. Pour sauce
over fish. Mix in peas, chopped egg and
parsley. Cook potatoes until soft. Mash, add
remaining butter and cream, and salt and
pepper and mix well. Fork mashed potato on
to fish mixture. Cook for 35 minutes at
180C (350F/Gas 4) until fish is hot through
and topping golden and crispy. Serve
immediately with a mixed leaf salad.

*Pesach friendly - Serves 10*

# — BAKED SALMON WITH LATKES —

450g (1lb) potatoes, grated
450g (1lb) courgettes (zucchini), grated
4 eggs, beaten
4 tablespoons plain (all-purpose) flour
3 cloves garlic, finely chopped
2 tablespoons fresh coriander (cilantro), finely
   chopped
2 teaspoons dried coriander
salt and freshly ground black pepper
150g (5oz) Cheddar cheese, grated
8 tablespoons vegetable oil
4 salmon fillets, about 175g (6oz) each, skinned and
   pin-boned
150ml (5fl oz/⅓ cup) dry white wine
extra virgin olive oil, for drizzling
fresh coriander (cilantro), to garnish

Preheat oven to 180C (350F/Gas 4). Make the latkes: remove excess water from grated potato and courgettes (zucchini) by squeezing dry in a clean tea towel or paper towels. This is best done in batches. Place potato and courgettes (zucchini) in a large bowl. Add eggs, flour, garlic, fresh coriander (cilantro), dried coriander, salt and pepper and cheese and mix very well. Divide into 12 portions.

Heat vegetable oil in a large frying pan (skillet). Place portions of mixture in pan. Flatten with a palette knife and cook for 4-5 minutes. Turn over and cook for a further 4 minutes. Try not to disturb them whilst cooking so that a good crust forms. (Change oil and clean pan out if it starts to burn and leaves black crumbs.)

Remove latkes and place on paper towels to drain. Place on a baking sheet lined with baking parchment, and cook in the oven for a final 10 minutes to crispen up.

Place the salmon into a deep casserole. Season with salt and pepper. Pour wine over and cook covered for about 20 minutes or until cooked: the flesh is no longer bright pink and is firm to touch.

To serve, place one latke on a warmed plate, then sit a salmon fillet on it and top with another latke. Drizzle some extra virgin olive oil over the salmon and plate. Garnish with some coriander leaves and serve with stir-fried pak choi (Chinese cabbage).

*Pesach friendly*
*Serves 6*

## ———— ORANGE HOT POT ————

6 tablespoons olive oil
900g (2lb) beef steak or shoulder of lamb, cubed
3 cloves garlic, finely chopped
300g (10oz) shallots, cut in half
300g (10oz) chestnut mushrooms, cut into quarters
1 aubergine (eggplant), cubed
1 orange pepper (capsicum), chopped
2 carrots, coarsely chopped
300ml (10fl oz/1¼ cups) red wine
1 tablespoon cinnamon
rind (zest) and juice of 1 orange
salt and freshly ground black pepper
2-3 sweet potatoes, finely sliced
3 tablespoons extra virgin olive oil

Preheat the oven to 160C (325F/Gas 3). Heat olive oil in a large saucepan and cook meat in batches until lightly browned. Set aside. In the same saucepan fry garlic and shallots until browned; set aside. Fry mushrooms and aubergine (eggplant) together in same pan until they are softened. Mix together meat, shallots, garlic, mushrooms and aubergine (eggplant). Add chopped pepper (capsicum) and carrots to meat mixture.

Transfer to an ovenproof serving dish and add red wine, cinnamon, orange rind (zest) and juice, and salt and pepper. Cover and cook in the oven for 1 hour. Remove from the oven and remove cover. Arrange thin slices of sweet potato on top of meat. Drizzle extra virgin olive oil over, season again and return to the oven for a further hour or until sweet potato is cooked and crispy.

*Pesach friendly*
*Serves 6*

# SESAME & ORANGE LAMB CHOPS

6 tablespoons sesame oil
rind (zest) and juice of 3 oranges
6 tablespoons red wine
3 teaspoons soft brown sugar
salt and freshly ground black pepper
6 large lamb chops
6 tablespoons vegetable oil
6 tablespoons sesame seeds, to garnish
STIR-FRIED GREENS
6 tablespoons vegetable oil
2 tablespoons sesame oil
1.35kg (3lb) mixed fresh green vegetables of your
   choice e.g. red chard, spinach, broccoli, curly kale
   and cabbage, finely shredded or chopped

Mix together sesame oil, orange rind (zest)
and juice, wine, sugar and salt and pepper to
make marinade. Marinate lamb for at least
2 hours or preferably overnight in the
refrigerator, turning from time to time.
Remove lamb from marinade and dry on
paper towels. Pour marinade into a
saucepan. Bring to a boil and reduce by one
third. Heat vegetable oil in a frying pan
(skillet) and fry chops for 4-5 minutes on
each side, until cooked to taste.

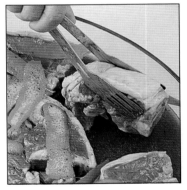

Toast sesame seeds in a dry saucepan until
they start to colour. Turn off the heat as
they will continue to cook until golden. Set
aside. Stir-fry greens; heat both oils in a wok
or large saucepan. Add greens and stir-fry
until cooked to taste. Put stir-fried greens on
to a large warmed serving plate. Arrange
chops on top. Spoon hot marinade over
each chop and sprinkle with toasted sesame
seeds.

*Serves 6*

# — CHICKEN & SEPHARDI RICE —

3 tablespoons olive oil
1 onion, finely chopped
3 cloves garlic, finely chopped
1 teaspoon ground cinnamon
300g (10oz/1¼ cups) basmati rice
1 litre (35fl oz/4½ cups) chicken stock
rind (zest) and juice of 1 orange
50g (2oz/⅓ cup) chopped dates
50g (2oz/½ cup) chopped dried apricots
6 boneless, skinless chicken breasts
6 tablespoons olive oil
salt and freshly ground black pepper
roasted blanched whole almonds, to garnish

Heat olive oil in a large saucepan and sauté onion and garlic until soft. Add cinnamon.

Add rice and cook, stirring, for 1 minute until translucent. Stir in stock, orange rind (zest) and juice, dates and apricots. Bring to a boil and simmer, covered, for about 12 minutes. When rice is just cooked, set pan aside for 10 minutes, covered. Preheat grill (broiler) to medium.

Baste chicken with olive oil, and season well with salt and pepper. Grill (broil) for 5 minutes on one side, then turn and cook for a further 5 minutes or until juices run clear when chicken is pierced with a knife. To serve, place a mound of pilaf in centre of each warmed plate. Slice each chicken breast at an angle and fan it on top of pilaf. Sprinkle with roasted almonds and serve immediately.

*Serves 6*

## SAFFRON LAMB TAGINE

6 tablespoons vegetable oil
900g (2lb) cubed shoulder of lamb
300g (10oz) shallots
4 garlic cloves, crushed
2cm (1in) fresh root ginger, finely chopped
4 teaspoons ground cinnamon
1 teaspoon cayenne pepper
½ teaspoon saffron threads
3 tablespoons plain (all-purpose) flour
400g (14oz) can chopped tomatoes
150ml (5fl oz/⅓ cup) red wine
900ml (32fl oz/4 cups) chicken stock
85g (3oz) dried cranberries
85g (3oz/½ cup) raisins
85g (3oz/¾ cup) shelled pistachio nuts
115g (4oz/1 cup) whole blanched almonds, roasted

Preheat the oven to 170C (325F/Gas 3).
Heat oil and sauté lamb in batches in a large
frying pan (skillet). Remove lamb and set
aside. Fry shallots and garlic until browned
and set aside. In the same pan, fry ginger,
cinnamon, cayenne and saffron for
1 minute. Stir in flour and cook for
1 minute. Add stock, tomatoes and wine
and stir well. Bring to a boil. There may
seem to be too much liquid but this will
reduce considerably during cooking.

Transfer lamb, onions, garlic and sauce to a
large casserole. Cook in the oven for 2-2½
hours. After 1 hour add half the cranberries
and all the raisins. Spoon the tagine in a
warmed serving dish, and scatter with
pistachios, almonds and remaining
cranberries. Serve with cous cous.

*Serves 8*

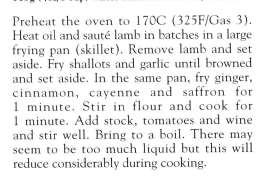

# –CHICKEN WITH WHISKY SAUCE–

1 roasting chicken, about 2kg (4½ lb), cut into
   6 portions
4 cloves garlic, crushed
6 sprigs rosemary
1 lemon, quartered
salt and freshly ground black pepper
5 tablespoons olive oil
2 tablespoons soft brown sugar
24 shallots or baby onions
320g (11oz) oyster mushrooms, sliced
SAUCE
320g (11oz) dried apricots, halved and soaked in
   200ml (7fl oz/scant 1 cup) whisky overnight
345g (12 oz/1 cup) apricot jam (preserve)
200ml (7fl oz/scant 1 cup) chicken stock
rind (zest) and juice of 1 lemon

Preheat oven to 200C (400F/Gas 6). Place
chicken pieces, skin side down, in a roasting
tin (pan) with 115ml (4fl oz/½ cup) water.
Scatter with half the garlic, the rosemary
sprigs and lemon quarters. Season with salt
and pepper. Drizzle 2 tablespoons olive oil
over and roast for 30 minutes. Turn chicken
over and roast for a further 1 hour. Heat
remaining olive oil and brown sugar in a
medium frying pan (skillet). Fry shallots
until golden brown.

Add oyster mushrooms and remaining
garlic. Continue to fry over a medium heat
for a further 5 minutes, until mushrooms
have softened and garlic is cooked. To make
sauce, put all the sauce ingredients in a
saucepan and reduce by one third over a
medium heat. Place a mound of mushroom
mixture on each warmed plate and top with
a piece of chicken. Pour sauce over. Serve
with wild rice.

*Serves 6*

# LAYERED SALMON FILLET

2 red and 2 yellow peppers (capsicums), halved
6 tablespoons olive oil
1 large aubergine (eggplant), sliced lengthwise
4½lb (2kg) whole salmon, skinned and cut into
　2 fillets
2 tablespoons black olive tapenade (olive paste) [omit
　for Pesach]
salt and freshly ground black pepper
50g (2oz) fresh basil, chopped
2 tablespoons extra virgin olive oil

Place red and yellow peppers (capsicums) on a baking sheet, skin side up. Brush with 3 tablespoons olive oil.

Grill (broil) peppers (capsicums) until skins blister. Transfer to a bowl and cover with clear film (plastic wrap). Once cooled, remove skin. Brush aubergine (eggplant) slices with remaining olive oil and grill (broil) until soft. Preheat the oven to 180C (350F/Gas 4). Cover a large baking sheet with baking parchment. Place a salmon fillet, skinned side down in centre. Spread with 1 tablespoon tapenade. Layer with half the aubergine (eggplant) slices, salt and pepper, half the basil and all the red peppers (capsicums).

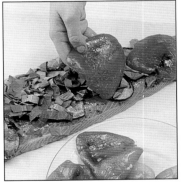

Continue layering with remaining aubergine (eggplant) and basil and all the yellow peppers (capsicums). Spread top of second salmon fillet with remaining tapenade. Place on top of stack, tapenade side down. Drizzle extra virgin olive oil over and season with salt and pepper. Wrap salmon stack with baking parchment and tie at three intervals with string. Bake for 50 minutes. Serve with pak choi and baby new potatoes.

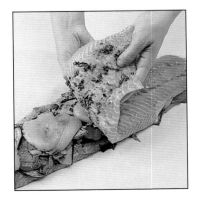

*Can be Parev. Pesach friendly*
*Serves 8*

# — TOFU & VEGETABLE STIR FRY —

115g (4oz) green and yellow patty pan squash
115g (4oz) baby plum tomatoes
7 tablespoons toasted sesame oil
200g (7oz) tofu, cut into 2.5cm (1in) pieces
5cm (2in) fresh root ginger, finely chopped
2 cloves garlic, crushed
2 red onions, sliced
2 red peppers (capsicums), sliced into strips
2 tablespoons hot vegetable stock
1 tablespoon clear honey
3 tablespoons satay sauce or peanut sauce
1 tablespoon hoisin sauce
1 tablespoon crunchy peanut butter
rind (zest) and juice of 1 lime
225g (8oz) baby spinach, roughly chopped
chopped fresh coriander (cilantro), to garnish

Cut patty pan squash and baby tomatoes in half. Heat a large wok or frying pan (skillet) with 4 tablespoons of sesame oil. Stir fry tofu, ginger, garlic, onion, red pepper (capsicum), patty pans and tomatoes for 5 minutes. Add hot vegetable stock. Stir and simmer for 1 minute.

Mix together honey, satay sauce, hoisin sauce, peanut butter and lime juice and add to wok. Continue to stir fry a further 3-5 minutes until vegetables are just cooked and evenly coated with peanut glaze. Add spinach and cook for a further 2 minutes. Transfer vegetables to a large warmed serving platter and keep warm. Scatter with lime rind (zest) and chopped coriander (cilantro). Serve with stir-fried crispy noodles.

*Can be Parev - Serves 6*

# — LIME SEABASS EN PAPILLOTES —

2 leeks, shredded
2 red onions, sliced
3 heads pak choi (chinese cabbage), finely shredded
1 red pepper (capsicum), chopped
115g (4oz) baby corn, sliced lengthwise
6 sea bass fillets, 150g (5oz) each, skinned
rind (zest) and juice of 3 limes
6 sprigs of lemon thyme
4 cloves garlic, crushed
2.5cm (1in) fresh ginger root, grated
15g (½oz) flat-leaf parsley
12 tablespoons white wine
6 tablespoons light soy sauce
3 tablespoons extra virgin olive oil
3 tablespoons sesame oil
freshly ground black pepper

Preheat oven to 200C (400F/Gas 6). Cut 6 foil rectangles large enough to wrap fish in with margin for folding edges. Place the foil rectangles on a baking sheet. Mix vegetables and divide them evenly between foil rectangles. Place a seabass fillet on top of each vegetable bed. Sprinkle rind (zest) and juice of limes over fish. Place a sprig of lemon thyme on top. Mix garlic, ginger, parsley, wine, soy sauce, olive oil and sesame oil together in a small bowl. Spoon over each fish. Season with pepper.

Seal papillotes by bringing up long edges to meet, and folding edges over twice. Fold ends over twice so that it forms a sealed parcel. Make sure all the foil edges are folded together tightly to secure all juices inside. Bake for 25 minutes. The parcels will puff up. Transfer papillotes to warmed plates and allow guests to open their own parcels. Serve with mashed potato.

*Serves 6*

# — CHEESE & COURGETTE PIE —

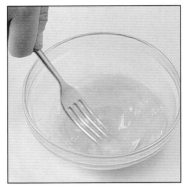

7 large eggs
375g (13oz/3¼ cups) plain (all-purpose) flour
200ml (7fl oz/scant 1 cup) olive oil
1kg (2lb) courgettes (zucchini), sliced lengthwise
2 red peppers (capsicums), quartered
2 yellow peppers (capsicums), quartered
300g (10oz/1⅓ cups) cream cheese
150g (5oz/⅔ cup) herb cream cheese
50g (2oz) Parmesan, grated
175g (6oz) mixed fresh herbs e.g. mint, basil, parsley,
  chopped
salt and freshly ground black pepper
1 egg yolk, for glazing
40g (1½oz) pine nuts

Lightly beat 2 of the eggs.

Make pastry by combining flour, 85ml
(3fl oz/⅓ cup) of the olive oil and beaten
eggs in a food processor. Gradually add 50ml
(2fl oz/¼ cup) water until a firm dough is
formed. Wrap in clear film (plastic wrap)
and refrigerate for at least 2 hours.

Brush courgettes (zucchini) with some of
the remaining olive oil and grill (broil) for
2 minutes on each side until golden. Skin
red and yellow peppers (capsicums) by
placing them on a baking sheet, brushing
them with remaining olive oil and grilling
(broiling) skin side up until skin blisters.
Immediately put peppers (capsicums) in a
bowl and cover with clear film (plastic
wrap). Remove skins when cool.

Using an electric mixer, beat both cream cheeses until smooth and well combined. Continue mixing, adding remaining eggs one at a time. Stir in grated Parmesan and chopped herbs and season to taste.

Preheat oven to 180C (350F/Gas 4). Cut off one-third of pastry to keep for top of pie. Roll out remaining pastry on a lightly floured surface, large enough to line a 23cm (9in) springform or loose bottomed tin (pan). Line tin (pan) with pastry, allowing it to hang over sides. Spread one third of cream cheese mixture over pastry base and top with half peppers (capsicums) and courgettes (zucchini). Repeat layering and finish with remaining third of cream cheese mixture.

Roll out remaining pastry into a circle. Place on top of pie, trim pastry and crimp edges together, sealing well. Re-roll pastry trimmings and cut into strips. Plait (braid) strips and place in a circle on top. Glaze with egg yolk. Bake for 45 minutes. Remove from oven and fill centre of pastry circle with pine nuts. Cook for a further 15-30 minutes until golden. Serve with spinach.

*Serves 8*

# – SALMON-STUFFED SOLE FILLETS –

350g (12oz) fresh salmon, boned and skinned
4 spring onions (scallions), roughly chopped
2.5cm (1in) fresh ginger root, roughly chopped
3 tablespoons chopped fresh dill
1 egg white
3 tablespoons whipping (heavy) cream
salt and freshly ground black pepper
12 fillets lemon sole or plaice, skinned

Place salmon, onions, ginger and dill in food processor and work to a paste. With machine running, pour egg white through feeder tube and blend for 30 seconds. Add cream in same way. Season to taste.

Spread mousseline evenly over each sole fillet and roll up from the thick end. Secure with a cocktail stick.

Place in a shallow frying pan (skillet) and pour in 150ml (5fl oz/⅔ cup) water. Cover pan and poach over a low heat for 10 minutes. Remove fish rolls from pan using a slotted spoon and drain on paper towels. Place 2 sole and salmon rolls, overlapping each other, on warmed plates. Remove cocktail sticks. Serve with mashed potato.

*Pesach friendly*
*Serves 6*

# CRISPY DUCK SALAD WITH FRUIT

5 cloves garlic, 4 sliced and 1 whole
5cm (2in) fresh root ginger, sliced
3 juniper berries
salt and freshly ground black pepper
2.25kg (5lb) duck, quartered
2 litres (70fl oz/9 cups) vegetable oil
175g (6oz) raspberries
1 teaspoon light muscovado sugar
2 tablespoons red wine vinegar
½ teaspoon Dijon mustard
5 tablespoons olive oil
300g (10oz) bag mixed salad leaves
115g (4oz) watercress
115g (4oz) beansprouts
85g (3oz) blueberries or blackcurrants
1 bunch chives, coarsely chopped

Fill a large saucepan with water and add the
sliced garlic, ginger, juniper berries, and salt
and pepper. Bring to a boil. Add duck.
Simmer, covered, for 45 minutes. Remove
duck and allow to cool slightly before
removing meat from bone, discarding skin.
Shred the meat into large strips. Heat oil in
a large pan, or deep fat fryer, until hot. Fry
strips of duck in batches, 1-2 minutes, until
crispy. Remove and drain on paper towels.
Keep hot.

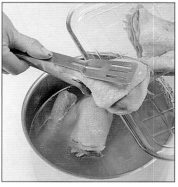

Put half the raspberries, the sugar, vinegar,
remaining garlic clove, mustard and olive
oil in a processor and process. Check
seasoning. Sieve to remove seeds.
Refrigerate until ready to serve. Arrange
salad leaves, bean sprouts, watercress and
fruit on individual large plates. Scatter the
strips of duck and chives over. Drizzle with
dressing and serve sprinkled with roasted
sesame seeds if you like.

*Serves 6 as a starter; 4 as a main course*

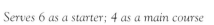

# — STUFFED SHOULDER OF LAMB —

1 slice of bread, toasted
1 tablespoon each chopped fresh parsley, rosemary
   and mint
300g (11oz) fresh spinach, chopped
1 tablespoon olive oil
2 shallots, chopped
2 cloves garlic, crushed
2 tablespoons raisins
3 tablespoons pine nuts, toasted
rind (zest) and juice of 1 orange
1 egg
salt and freshly ground black pepper
2kg (4½lb) boned shoulder of lamb
300 ml (10 fl oz/1¼ cups) red wine
4 sprigs rosemary
1 tablespoon soft brown sugar

Process toast and herbs in a food processor until crumbed. Cook spinach in a dry pan until wilted. Drain well and set aside. Heat olive oil in a large frying pan (skillet) and sauté shallots until softened. Add garlic and cook for a further 2 minutes. Add spinach, raisins, toasted pine nuts, breadcrumb mixture, orange rind (zest), egg and salt and pepper to the pan and mix well. Remove from heat.

Preheat oven to 200C (400F/Gas 6). Unroll meat and season lightly. Spread top of meat with spinach stuffing. Fold in two longer sides towards centre and secure with string to make an elongated parcel.

Place lamb parcel in a roasting tin (pan).
Pour over 300ml (10fl oz/1¼ cups) boiling
water, half the red wine and the orange
juice. Season and add rosemary. Roast,
covered, for 30 minutes. Baste meat with
juices.

Lower temperature to 190C (375F/Gas 5)
for about 1 hour according to how well done
you like the meat, uncovering for the last
30 minutes. Remove lamb from the oven.
Cover and leave for 10 minutes to rest.
Remove from tin (pan), cut away string and
carve into thick slices.

Pour some of the excess fat from roasting tin
(pan) and discard. To make gravy, deglaze
roasting tin (pan) by adding remaining red
wine and soft brown sugar to juices. Bring to
a boil and reduce by a third until it begins to
thicken a little, stirring constantly. Serve
slices of lamb with gravy and with roast
potatoes.

*Serves 8*

# HONEY GLAZED CHICKEN BREAST

4 tablespoons clear honey
425ml (15fl oz/scant 2 cups) fruity red wine
6 boneless, skinless chicken breasts
salt and freshly ground black pepper
115g (4oz/2 cups) fresh white breadcrumbs [matzoh meal for Pesach]
large bunch chives, finely chopped
4 eggs, beaten
6 tablespoons vegetable or groundnut (peanut) oil
bunch watercress, to garnish

Preheat oven to 200C (400F/Gas 6). Simmer honey and wine together in a medium saucepan, uncovered, for 10 minutes. Set glaze aside.

Lightly season chicken breasts with salt and pepper. Mix breadcrumbs and chives in a shallow dish. Dip each breast in egg and coat with breadcrumb and chive mixture.

Heat oil in a large frying pan (skillet). Fry each coated chicken breast until evenly browned on both sides. Place chicken in a shallow roasting tin (pan). Pour one third of honey glaze over. Cook for 8-10 minutes in oven. Pour over a further third of the glaze. Return to oven. Cook for 10-15 minutes. Cut chicken at an angle and fan it on serving plates. Spoon remaining glaze over and garnish with watercress. Serve with cous cous or wild rice.

*Pesach friendly (chicken only) - Serves 6*

# – CHICKEN & GARLIC POTATOES –

900g (2lb) new potatoes cut into 2.5cm (1in) chunks
300ml (10fl oz/½ cup) olive oil
350g (12oz) tomatoes, skinned and cut into chunks
200g (7oz) small onions, halved
3 cloves garlic, finely chopped
8 sprigs thyme
8 sprigs sage
salt and freshly ground black pepper
85g (3oz) pitted black olives
6 tablespoons groundnut (peanut) or vegetable oil
6 boneless, skinless chicken breasts
20g (¾oz) parsley, finely chopped

Place potatoes in a saucepan and cover with cold, salted water; bring to a boil and simmer for 5 minutes. Drain well.

Preheat oven to 190C (375F/Gas 5). Put olive oil in a large frying pan (skillet) over a medium heat. Add potatoes, tomatoes, onions, garlic, thyme and sage. Season well and simmer for 15 minutes. Transfer to a casserole dish. Cook, covered, in the oven for 1 hour or until potatoes are cooked through. Add olives during last 15 minutes of cooking.

Meanwhile, heat groundnut (peanut) oil in a large frying pan (skillet) until hot. Season chicken fillets. Fry in batches for 3-4 minutes on each side until browned. Slice each fillet into four. Place chicken in a covered ovenproof dish with 115ml (4fl oz/½ cup) water and put in oven 15 minutes before potatoes are done. To serve, stir chopped parsley gently through potato mixture and spoon on to warmed plates. Arrange chicken slices on top.

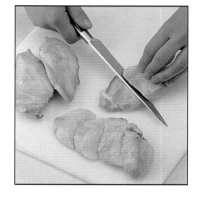

*Can be Parev. Pesach friendly - Serves 6*

# ROLLED SPICED BEEF

6 tablespoons olive oil
450g (1lb) brown cap mushrooms, peeled and finely
    chopped
6 cloves garlic, crushed
salt and freshly ground black pepper
1 slice white bread
1 teaspoon peppercorns
6 juniper berries
4 teaspoons Chinese five-spice powder
2 teaspoons coriander seeds
4 tablespoons plain (all-purpose) flour
4 slices prime Bola or sliced braising steak, about
    160g (5½oz) each, flattened
3 tablespoons vegetable oil
570ml (20fl oz) fruity red wine

Heat 2 tablespoons olive oil in a large
saucepan until hot. Add mushrooms and
garlic and cook until juices are absorbed.
Season with salt and pepper. Process
mushrooms and bread together. Place all the
spices and flour in a pestle and mortar and
crush to a coarse powder. Brush flattened
steaks with remaining olive oil and coat
them on both sides with spice mixture.
Spread mushroom mixture thickly on to
steaks along length. Roll meat lengthwise
and tie with string in several places to make
a long parcel.

Preheat oven to 160C (325F/Gas 3). Heat
vegetable oil in a large frying pan (skillet).
Brown beef parcels, one at a time to seal the
meat quickly. Remove beef parcels and
place in a large casserole. Pour red wine
over and cook in the oven for 2½ hours.
Cut away string and slice beef into rounds.
Arrange  on warmed plates in a crescent
shape. Spoon red wine juices over beef and
serve immediately.

*Serves 4*

# AUBERGINE SCHNITZEL

450g (1lb) white bread
6 tablespoons chopped fresh parsley
3-4 aubergines (eggplants), cut lengthwise into 0.5cm
  (¼in) slices
6 eggs, lightly beaten
115ml (4fl oz/½ cup) vegetable oil
450g (1lb) plum tomatoes, sliced
4 tablespoons extra virgin olive oil, plus extra for
  drizzling
6 cloves garlic, finely chopped
salt and freshly ground black pepper
115g (4oz) Gruyère cheese, grated

Preheat oven to 200C (400F/Gas 6). Process
bread and parsley in a food processor.

Dip slices of aubergine (eggplant) in egg,
then breadcrumb mixture. Repeat to coat
well. Heat a large frying pan (skillet) with
4 tablespoons of the vegetable oil. Add
more oil as required. Fry aubergines
(eggplants) for 2 minutes on each side until
browned. Drain on paper towels. Place
tomatoes on a baking sheet. Sprinkle with
the extra virgin olive oil, chopped garlic,
salt and  pepper. Bake tomatoes for
15 minutes.

Cut each aubergine (eggplant) slice in half
on the diagonal and place on a baking sheet
lined with baking parchment. Place 4-5
slices of tomato on each half slice. Sprinkle
grated Gruyère cheese and salt and pepper
over, and drizzle with extra virgin olive oil.
Cover with another half slice. Repeat the
filling, and top with a third half slice.
Skewer each stack with two cocktail sticks
to secure. Bake for 15 minutes. Serve with a
pesto and mixed salad leaves.

*Serves 6*

# -TOMATO & FETA BREAD SALAD-

200ml (7fl oz/scant 1 cup) extra virgin olive oil
3 tablespoons red wine vinegar
4 cloves garlic, crushed to a paste
salt and freshly ground black pepper
350g (12oz) crusty bread or left-over challah, cubed
320g (11oz) red cherry tomatoes, cut in half, or salad
   tomatoes cut into wedges
320g (11oz) yellow cherry tomatoes (if available or
   use red), cut in half
150g (5oz) black olives, sliced in half
25g (1oz) fresh basil, finely chopped
200g (7oz) feta cheese, cubed

Put olive oil, vinegar, garlic paste, salt and
plenty of pepper into your serving bowl.
Add bread and mix.

Add tomatoes, olives, basil and feta cheese.
Toss to combine well, taking care not to
break up feta. Let salad stand at room
temperature for at least 15 minutes to allow
bread to soak up dressing. Serve with a
green salad that includes baby spinach
leaves, rocket (arugula) or watercress.

*Serves 6*

# SPICY FISH CAKES

450g (1lb) cod or other white fish fillet skinned,
  boned and cubed
milk, for poaching [soya milk for Parev]
4 spring onions (scallions)
2 red chillies, deseeded and chopped
2 cloves garlic, peeled
2cm (1in) fresh ginger root, finely chopped
25g (1oz) fresh coriander (cilantro)
250g (9oz) white bread
1 egg white, lightly whisked
salt and freshly ground black pepper
4 tablespoons shredded coconut
vegetable oil, for deep frying
115g (4oz/1 cup) plain (all-purpose) flour
2 eggs, lightly beaten

Put cubed fish into a shallow pan and cover
with milk. Bring to a boil and simmer for 3-
4 minutes. Strain fish reserving 50ml
(4fl oz/¼ cup) milk. Process fish in a food
processor with spring onions (scallions),
chillies, garlic, ginger, half the coriander
(cilantro), half the bread, the egg white, salt
and pepper, and reserved milk until mixed
but not puréed. Stir in coconut. With
floured hands, shape mixture into round
cakes using about 2 tablespoons each. Put
on a floured plate and chill in the fridge for
1 hour.

Process the remaining bread and remaining
coriander (cilantro) in a food processor.
Heat oil in a deep-fat fryer. Coat each fish
cake in flour, beaten egg and breadcrumb
mixture. Deep-fry fish cakes for 3-4 minutes
until golden. Drain on paper towels. Serve
with stir-fried vegetables and a wedge of
lime.

*Can be Parev*
*Serves 6*

# — BASQUE-STYLE TUNA STEW —

6 tablespoons olive oil
2 onions, roughly chopped
1 each red and yellow pepper (capsicum), chopped
1 large aubergine (eggplant), cubed
1 tablespoon paprika
400g (14oz) can chopped tomatoes
2 tablespoons sun-dried tomatoes, chopped
4 cloves garlic, sliced
150ml (5fl oz/⅔ cup) red wine
4 Desirée potatoes, cubed
1 unwaxed lemon, cut into quarters
2 sprigs lemon thyme
850ml (30fl oz/3¾ cups) vegetable stock
salt and freshly ground black pepper
800g (1¾lb) fresh tuna, cubed
1 small jar anchovies, drained

Heat olive oil in a large, heavy-based saucepan. Sauté onions and peppers (capsicums) for 5 minutes. Add aubergine (eggplant) and continue cooking until all vegetables are softened. Add paprika. Stir over heat for 30 seconds. Add tomatoes with their juice, chopped sun-dried tomatoes, sliced garlic, red wine, potatoes, lemon, lemon thyme, stock and salt and pepper to taste.  (Remember anchovies are salty.)

Simmer, uncovered, over a medium heat for about 20 minutes until potatoes are tender. Stir in tuna and anchovies. Cook for a further 2 minutes. Remove from the heat. Cover tuna stew and allow to stand for 5 minutes before checking seasoning and serving. Ladle into deep bowls and serve with chunks of crusty bread.

*Can be Parev*
*Serves 6*

# FISH & VEGETABLE PASTA

1 red pepper (capsicum), roughly chopped
1 yellow pepper (capsicum), roughly chopped
1 red onion, chopped into large chunks
6 tablespoons olive oil
4 cloves garlic, crushed
salt and freshly ground black pepper
300g (10oz) dried pasta shapes
150g (5oz) sugar snap peas
115g (4oz) asparagus, cut into 5cm (2in) lengths
85g (3oz) broad (fava) beans, fresh or frozen
4 smoked fish fillets, about 150g (5oz) each, skinned
and cut into bite-size pieces

Preheat oven to 200C (400F/Gas 6). Place peppers (capsicums) and onion in a roasting tin (pan) and drizzle with olive oil. Sprinkle with crushed garlic and salt and pepper. Roast for 15-20 minutes. Bring a large pan of salted water to a boil. Add dried pasta and cook according to package instructions. When pasta is al dente (firm to the bite), drain and transfer to a large serving dish.

Steam, blanch or microwave sugar snaps and asparagus until just cooked. Drain and plunge into cold water and drain again. Cook broad (fava) beans in boiling water for 2 minutes. Drain and remove the skins. Mix roasted vegetables and all their juices, sugar snaps, asparagus and broad (fava) beans into pasta. Season to taste. Mix in fish carefully to prevent it from breaking up. Serve hot, warm or cold.

*Can be Parev*
*Serves 4*

# — CHICKEN COUS COUS SALAD —

1 red pepper (capsicum), cut into 8 pieces
1 yellow pepper (capsicum), cut into 8 pieces
1 butternut squash, cut into small cubes
1 red onion, cut into large segments
olive oil, for drizzling
3 cloves garlic, finely chopped
salt and freshly ground black pepper
550ml (20fl oz/2½ cups) stock
350g (12oz) cous cous
4 cooked chicken breasts, sliced
225g (8oz) fresh peas
225g (8oz) asparagus, cut into 2.5cm (1in) lengths
    and cooked
4 tablespoons olive oil
rind (zest) and juice of 1 lime
3 tablespoons finely chopped fresh mint

Preheat the oven to 200C (400F/Gas 6).
Place red and yellow peppers (capsicums),
butternut squash and red onion in a roasting
tin (pan). Drizzle with olive oil (see above).
Sprinkle chopped garlic over. Season well
with salt and pepper. Roast for 20 minutes,
turn vegetables over and return to the oven
for a further 10 minutes. Heat stock in a
pan. Place cous cous into a heat resistant
bowl and pour hot stock over. Cover with
clear film (plastic wrap) and leave for 10
minutes for grains to swell. Fluff up with a
fork and set aside.

Mix cooked chicken with roasted
vegetables, raw fresh peas, cooked asparagus
and cous cous. Combine olive oil, rind
(zest) and juice of lime and mint together
and pour over chicken cous cous salad.
Serve at room temperature.

*Serves 6*

# ——PAN-FRIED CALVES' LIVER——

4 slices calves' or ox liver
cooking salt, for sprinkling
900g (2lb) potatoes, chopped
150g (5oz) margarine
2 tablespoons whole grain mustard
salt and freshly ground black pepper
4 tablespoons plain (all-purpose) flour or fine matzoh
    meal
4 tablespoons olive oil
flat-leaf parsley, to garnish

To Kosher the liver: wash the liver. Place
on foil in a grill (broiler) pan. Sprinkle with
cooking salt. Grill (broil) until liver changes
colour.

Turn over and grill (broil) other side. Rinse
off any excess salt. [Discard foil after use as
this is not Kosher.] Cook potatoes in
boiling, salted water until tender. Drain and
return to hot empty pan. Mash using a fork,
masher or ricer until potatoes are soft,
creamy and free from lumps. Gradually add
85g (3oz) margarine, mustard and salt and
pepper, mixing well. Keep mash warm.

Season flour with salt and pepper. Coat liver
with seasoned flour. Melt remaining
margarine together with oil until fat starts
to foam. Fry liver for about 3 minutes on
each side. Spoon some mash on to a warmed
plate. Place a slice of liver on top of the
mash and garnish with flat-leaf parsley.

*Liver: Pesach friendly*
*Mustard mashed potato: Can be Parev*
*Serves 4*

# –PAPPARDELLE & SMOKED DUCK–

2 fennel bulbs, roughly chopped
3 tablespoons olive oil
5 oranges
450g (1lb) pappardelle pasta
3 tablespoons extra virgin olive oil
salt and freshly ground black pepper
6 thick slices of smoked duck, cut into bite-size cubes
bunch of chives, chopped into 1cm (½in) lengths
large bunch watercress, stalks removed
grated soya Parmesan (optional)

Preheat the oven to 200C (400F/Gas 6). Place fennel in a roasting tin (pan) and drizzle with olive oil; roast for 20 minutes.

Remove rind (zest) from 4 of the oranges. Peel the 4 oranges, removing pith. Using a sharp knife, cut between membranes and remove orange segments. Cook pasta according to the package instructions. Drain. Return pasta to pan. Toss pasta in juice of remaining orange and extra virgin olive oil. Season well with salt and pepper.

Add cubed duck, roasted fennel, segmented oranges and orange rind (zest), chopped chives and trimmed watercress. Mix well. Serve immediately in a large bowl. Sprinkle some soya Parmesan over, if using.

**Variation:** For a vegetarian option, omit duck and add 225g (8oz) cooked asparagus and 115g (4oz) feta cheese.

*Serves 6*

# PECAN CHICKEN SALAD

2 slices of white bread [85g (3oz) matzoh meal for
  Pesach]
200g (7oz) pecan nuts
4 boneless, skinless chicken breasts
2 large eggs, beaten
4 tablespoons groundnut (peanut) or vegetable oil
large bunch fresh basil
115ml (4fl oz/½ cup) extra virgin olive oil
1 tablespoon balsamic vinegar
salt and freshly ground black pepper
200g (7oz) new potatoes, cut in half
225g (8oz) asparagus, chopped into 2.5cm (1in)
  lengths but leaving spears intact
200g (7oz) mixed salad leaves
3 small avocados, sliced

Preheat oven to 200C (400F/Gas 6). Process
bread and pecans in food processor. Dip
chicken breasts into beaten egg followed by
breadcrumb mixture. Repeat process to give
a thick coating. Heat groundnut (peanut)
oil in a frying pan (skillet). Fry chicken for
2-3 minutes on each side until browned.
Remove chicken breasts from pan and place
on a baking sheet lined with baking
parchment. Complete cooking in the oven
for 15 minutes.

Finely chop basil in a food processor or
blender. Add olive oil, balsamic vinegar,
salt and pepper. Boil potatoes, drain and
return them to pan. Cover with basil
dressing, mix and set aside. Steam asparagus
until just cooked. Mix potatoes, salad leaves
and asparagus. Place salad on individual
plates. Slice chicken. Arrange chicken and
avocado slices alternately in a semi-circle.
Drizzle any excess dressing over and serve.

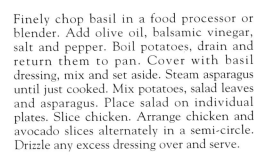

*Pesach friendly*
*Serves 6*

# CRISPY TURKEY LOAF

1-2 tablespoons olive oil
1 red onion, roughly chopped
2 courgette (zucchini), sliced
outer leaves of 1 savoy cabbage, stalks removed
450g (1lb) minced (ground) turkey
2 slices white bread, crumbled [75g (3oz) matzoh
   meal for Pesach]
1 egg
2 tablespoons redcurrant jelly
1 bunch fresh mint
2 tablespoons sun-dried tomato purée
salt and freshly ground black pepper
3 salad tomatoes, sliced

Preheat the oven to 190C (375F/Gas 5).
Heat some olive oil in a frying pan (skillet)
and sauté onion until softened. Remove
onion and set aside. Add more olive oil if
needed and lightly fry courgettes (zucchini)
for 30 seconds on each side. Line a 900g
(2lb) loaf tin with cabbage leaves, leaving
enough overhang to cover loaf tin. Put
minced (ground) turkey, bread, egg,
redcurrant jelly, fresh mint, tomato purée
and sautéed onion in a food processor.
Season generously with salt and pepper.
Process to a paste.

Spoon half turkey mixture into prepared
loaf tin. Layer courgettes (zucchini) on top
of turkey, followed by tomatoes. Spoon
remaining turkey mixture on top and level.
Fold overhanging cabbage leaves over.
Cover with greased foil. Bake for 50 minutes
or until firm to touch. Drain any excess
liquid. Discard foil and invert on to an
ovenproof platter. Return to oven for
10 minutes. Slice and serve with jacket
potatoes and tomato salsa.

*Use for Pesach - Serves 6*

# — CHICKEN MASALA WITH RICE —

4 boneless, skinless chicken breasts
salt
MARINADE
juice of 1 lemon
juice of 1 lime
2 cloves garlic, finely sliced
1 teaspoon medium-hot curry powder
1 tablespoon chilli oil
2 tablespoons clear honey
2 tablespoons chopped fresh coriander (cilantro),
  plus extra leaves, to garnish
RICE
300g (10oz) basmati rice
4 saffron threads
½ teaspoon turmeric
vegetable oil, for greasing

Combine marinade ingredients with 1 teaspoon salt. Pour over chicken and leave for at least 2 hours or overnight in the refrigerator. Preheat the oven to 180C (350F/Gas 4). Put rice, 1 teaspoon salt and 550ml (20fl oz/2½ cups) water in a saucepan and bring to a boil. Add turmeric and saffron. Simmer for 10-15 minutes, until water is absorbed and rice is soft. Check seasoning. Grease 6 timbales with vegetable oil. Fill with cooked rice. Cut 6 foil circles to act as lids, grease with vegetable oil and seal over each timbale.

Sit timbales in a large roasting tin (pan) half filled with boiling water (bain-marie). Place bain-marie in oven and cook for 10-15 minutes. Grill chicken for 15-20 minutes until golden, basting occasionally with marinade. Slice chicken at an angle and fan slices out on each plate. Place a timbale of rice next to it. Garnish with coriander (cilantro) and serve with mango chutney and sautéed fresh vegetables.

*Serves 6*

# — RASPBERRY CHEESECAKES —

butter, for greasing
5 tablespoons caster (superfine) sugar, plus extra for
  dusting
700g (1½lb/3 cups) ricotta [cream cheese for Pesach]
3 eggs, separated
1 tablespoon plain (all-purpose) flour [potato flour
  for Pesach]
rind (zest) of 2 lemons
juice of 1 lemon
seeds from a vanilla pod or 1 teaspoon vanilla essence
  (extract)
375g (13oz) fresh raspberries
icing (confectioners') sugar, for dusting
115g (4oz) toasted flaked almonds
fresh mint, to decorate

Preheat the oven to 190C (375F/Gas 5).
Grease base and sides of 8 ramekins with
butter and line bases with circles of baking
parchment. Dust inside each with caster
(superfine) sugar, shaking out excess. Beat
together ricotta cheese, sugar, egg yolks,
flour, lemon rind (zest), lemon juice and
vanilla seeds or essence (extract). Whisk egg
whites until stiff peaks form. Fold one
spoonful of egg white into ricotta mixture
using a large metal spoon. Fold in remainder
gently. Spoon mixture into each ramekin to
half fill.

Divide 250g (9oz) raspberries between
ramekins. Spoon remaining ricotta mixture
on top. Place in a roasting tin (pan) filled
with boiling water (bain marie) in the oven
for 35 minutes. Turn off oven and leave
cheesecakes to cool in oven for 1 hour.
Chill in fridge for at least 2 hours or
overnight. Invert on to plates, peel off
baking parchment and dust with icing
(confectioners') sugar. Decorate with
almonds, mint and remaining raspberries.

*Pesach friendly - Serves 8*

# – FRUITS OF THE FOREST BRULÉE –

550ml (20fl oz/2½ cups) double (heavy) cream
1 cinnamon stick or 1 teaspoon ground cinnamon
3 egg yolks
50g (2oz/¼ cup) caster (superfine) sugar
25g (1oz) cornflour (cornstarch) or potato flour
450g (1lb) fresh or frozen summer fruits, thawed and
    drained if frozen
8 tablespoons icing (confectioners') sugar, or to taste
4 tablespoons dark soft brown sugar, or to taste

Bring the double (heavy) cream to a boil
with cinnamon in a large saucepan. Set
mixture aside for 10 minutes. Remove and
discard cinnamon stick.

Whisk together egg yolks, caster (superfine)
sugar and cornflour (cornstarch) until pale
and thick. Pour cream into egg mixture and
whisk to combine. Return mixture to the
saucepan. Stir over a moderate heat for 5-10
minutes until mixture thickens and coats
back of a wooden spoon. Do not boil.
Divide summer fruits equally between 6
ramekins. Sieve thickened cream into a
large jug. Carefully pour into each ramekin.
Leave mixture to chill in the fridge for at
least 4 hours or overnight.

Completely cover each ramekin with icing
(confectioners') sugar. Place under a hot
grill (broiler) for 2-3 minutes, or until sugar
has melted and is bubbling on top. Remove
immediately. Completely cover with dark
soft brown sugar. Grill (broil) again until
topping is shiny and caramelized. Chill for
at least 1 hour before serving.

*Pesach friendly*
*Serves 6*

# – APPLE & BLACKBERRY BASKETS –

85g (3oz/6 tablespoons) butter or margarine
3 tablespoons pure clear honey
225g (8oz/1 cup) soft brown sugar
6 Granny Smith apples, peeled and sliced
2-3 tablespoons cornflour (cornstarch)
filo pastry sheets, to make 24 squares 15 x 15cm
  (6 x 6in) each
115g (4oz/½ cup) unsalted butter or margarine, melted
115g (4oz) fresh blackberries
icing (confectioners') sugar, for dusting

Preheat oven to 200C (400F/Gas 6). Melt butter or margarine with honey and sugar in a saucepan. Bring to a boil and simmer for 5 minutes until it starts to caramelize.

Add sliced apples, lower the heat and cook for a further 3 minutes. Allow to cool. Strain off liquid and reserve. Mix cornflour (cornstarch) with 1 tablespoon of apple liquid and then stir into remaining liquid. Simmer for 2-3 minutes until it thickens. Cut filo pastry sheets into 24 squares 15 x 15cm (6 x 6in) each. Brush one filo square with melted butter. Place second square on top and brush again with melted butter. Place third square of filo on top. Repeat with all filo squares making 8 stacks of squares.

Brush four ramekins with melted butter. In each ramekin, put one filo stack and then place a second stack at an angle, leaving pointed edges long. Cover with foil and insert baking beans; bake blind for about 15 minutes. Fill with caramelized apples and sprinkle some blackberries on top. Heat apple liquid and place in centre of a plate, sit a filled basket on top, and dust with icing (confectioners') sugar.

*Can be Parev*
*Serves 4*

# — BREAD & BUTTER PUDDING —

250ml (9fl oz/1 cup) full-fat milk
250ml (9fl oz/1 cup) double (heavy) cream
1 vanilla pod, split lengthwise
40g (1½oz/3 tablespoons) butter, softened
3 large eggs
150g (5oz) caster (superfine) sugar
12 slices challah
50g (2oz) sultanas
2 tablespoons Cointreau
50g (2oz/2 tablespoons) apricot jam (preserve)
icing (confectioners') sugar, for dusting

Place sultanas in a small bowl and spoon the Cointreau over. Leave to soak. Preheat the oven to 180C (350F/Gas 4).

Put milk, cream and vanilla in a large saucepan. Bring to a boil. Remove from heat and infuse for 10 minutes. Grease a medium oval dish. Butter challah slices. Line base of dish with bread, buttered side down. Sprinkle bread evenly with soaked sultanas. Whisk eggs and sugar together until pale and thick. Remove split vanilla pod from milk. Add milk mixture to egg mixture and whisk briefly until just combined. Pour custard over bread and leave for 5 minutes to let it soak in.

Place dish in a roasting tin and fill it with boiling water to come half way up the oval dish (bain-marie). Bake for 35 minutes. Melt and sieve apricot jam (preserve) to make a glaze. Brush top of pudding with glaze. Dust with icing (confectioners') sugar. Put dish under a hot grill (broiler) until the top is golden brown. Dust again with icing (confectioners') sugar and serve.

*Serves 6*

# SOFT FRUIT TART

**PASTRY**
150g (5oz/⅔ cup) butter, softened
250g (9oz/2¼ cups) plain (all-purpose) flour
40g (1½oz) caster (superfine) sugar
rind (zest) of 1 lemon
1 tablespoon lemon juice
1 egg
1 egg yolk, beaten, for glazing
**FILLING** [for Parev, see opposite]
150ml (5fl oz/⅔ cup) fromage frais 0% fat
3 tablespoons icing (confectioners') sugar
**TOPPING**
soft seasonal fruits e.g. apricots, plums, peaches,
    nectarines, strawberries, dates etc.
1 jar apricot jam (preserve), warmed

Preheat the oven to 200C (400F/Gas 6). Put
all pastry ingredients in a food processor.
Process until a ball of dough has formed.
Flatten and wrap in clear film (plastic
wrap). Refrigerate for 30 minutes. Roll
pastry out on a lightly floured surface to fit a
25cm (10in) loose-bottomed tart tin (pan).
Line tin (pan) with pastry. Cover pastry
with foil (including edges) and fill with
baking beans; bake blind for 20 minutes.

Remove foil and baking beans and glaze
pastry with beaten egg yolk. Return to oven
for 5 minutes or until golden brown. Melt
and sieve apricot jam (preserve). Brush
warm jam (preserve) over pastry. Prepare
fruit as if for fruit salad. Mix filling
ingredients and spread on to cooled pastry
case. Add the soft fruits, and brush with
apricot jam (preserve).

**Parev alternative:** Use margarine in place of butter in the pastry.

FILLING
3 egg yolks
70g (2½oz) caster (superfine) sugar
20g (¾oz) plain (all-purpose) flour
250ml (9fl oz/1 cup) soya cream
1 split vanilla pod or 1 teaspoon vanilla essence (extract)
1 tablespoon custard powder

Beat eggs and sugar together until pale and thick. Bring soya cream to boil with split vanilla pod or essence (extract). Take 1 tablespoon of cream and mix with custard powder to form a paste. Whisk remaining cream into the custard paste. Pour custard cream into the egg and sugar mixture. Mix together.

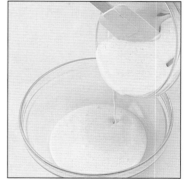

Return to saucepan. Heat gently, stirring continuously, until very thick. Remove the vanilla pod. Spoon warm filling into pastry case and spread evenly. Leave to cool. Place layer of clear film (plastic wrap) over filling to prevent a skin forming. Add the soft fruits, and brush with apricot glaze.

*Can be Parev*
*Serves 8-10*

# —— LACY VANILLA APPLE PIE ——

300g (10oz/2½ cups) plain (all-purpose) flour
160g (5½oz) cold butter or margarine
3 tablespoons caster (superfine) sugar
1 egg
1 teaspoon vanilla essence (extract)
FILLING
4-5 apples, sliced
2 teaspoons ground cinnamon
rind (zest) of 1 large orange
1 teaspoon plain (all-purpose) flour
3 tablespoons white sugar
30g (1oz) cold unsalted butter or margarine, cut into small pieces
orange juice, for glazing
caster (superfine) sugar, for sprinkling

Preheat the oven to 180C (350F/Gas 4). Put flour and butter in a food processor and process until mixture resembles breadcrumbs. Pulse in sugar. Add egg and vanilla essence (extract) and process until dough leaves sides of bowl. Bring dough together into a ball and flatten with your hands. Wrap in clear film (plastic wrap) and refrigerate for 30 minutes. Reserve one-third of dough for lid. Roll out two-thirds of pastry and line a 22cm (9in) deep loose-bottomed pie dish.

Mix apples with cinnamon, orange rind (zest), flour and sugar and coat well. Transfer to prepared pie dish. Dot with butter. Roll out remaining pastry. Cut into 1cm (½in) strips. Arrange half of strips across pie, leaving a 1cm (½in) gap between each. Repeat at right angles. Trim overlap. Press edges to seal. Glaze with orange juice and sprinkle with caster (superfine) sugar. Bake for 30-40 minutes until pastry is browned and juice is bubbling. Cool slightly before serving.

*Can be Parev - Serves 6*

# — HOT CHOCOLATE SOUFFLÉ —

50g (2oz/¼ cup) unsalted butter or margarine
5 tablespoons caster (superfine) sugar, plus extra for
  dusting
115g (4oz) plain (dark) chocolate
5 egg yolks
6 egg whites
icing (confectioners') sugar, for dusting
cocoa powder, for dusting

Preheat the oven to 200C (400F/Gas 6). Put a baking sheet, large enough to hold 6 ramekins, into the oven to preheat. Grease 6 ramekins with butter or margarine and then dust with caster (superfine) sugar.

Make sugar syrup by dissolving caster (superfine) sugar in 2 tablespoons water. Boil until syrupy, about 5 minutes. Melt chocolate in a bowl over a saucepan of simmering water or in the microwave. Stir in egg yolks. Add sugar syrup and mix. Beat egg whites until they form soft peaks. Add 1 tablespoon beaten egg white to chocolate mixture and fold in using a metal spoon.

Fold in remaining egg whites. Spoon mixture into individual ramekins until three-quarters full. Put ramekins on the preheated baking sheet. Place in the oven and cook for 10 minutes. Serve immediately; place ramekins on serving plates and dust with icing (confectioners') sugar and cocoa powder.

*Pesach friendly. Can be Parev*
*Serves 6*

# — CHOCOLATE BAKED ALASKAS —

85g (3oz) butter or margarine
225g (8oz) digestive [or Pesach] biscuits
2 tablespoons plain (dark) chocolate drops
570ml (20fl oz) chocolate ice cream [non-dairy
   equivalent for Parev]
4 egg whites
pinch of salt
200g (8oz) caster (superfine) sugar
cocoa powder, for dusting

Line a baking sheet with baking parchment.
Melt butter or margarine. Place biscuits and
chocolate drops in a food processor and
process. Stir in hot melted butter.

Continue processing until combined. Using
a 6cm (2½in) round pastry cutter as a
template, press the mixture into 8 rounds on
the baking sheet. Freeze for 10 minutes. Dip
an ice-cream scoop into hot water. Scoop a
ball of ice-cream on to each biscuit base.
Return baking sheet to freezer for at least
1 hour.

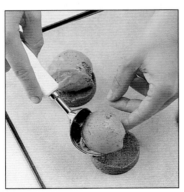

Whisk egg whites and salt until very stiff.
Add sugar, 1 tablespoon at a time, whisking
after each spoonful. The mixture should be
thick and glossy. Spoon or pipe a thick layer
of meringue to cover the base and ice cream
of each Alaska. Return to freezer for at least
4 hours or overnight. Bake Alaskas at 220C
(425F/Gas 7) for 5-7 minutes until golden.
Serve immediately dusted with cocoa
powder.

*Can be Parev. Pesach friendly*
*Serves 8*

# CRUNCHY NUT BISCOTTI

250g (9oz) plain (all-purpose) flour
250g (9oz) caster (superfine) sugar
½ teaspoon baking powder
50g (2oz) dried apricots, roughly chopped
50g (2oz) pitted dates, roughly chopped
50g (2oz) shelled pistachio nuts
50g (2oz) whole blanched almonds, roughly chopped
50g (2oz) skinned hazelnuts (filberts), roughly chopped
rind (zest) of 1 lemon
2 eggs, lightly beaten

Preheat the oven to 180C (350F/Gas 4). Mix flour, sugar and baking powder in a large bowl.

Add dried fruit, nuts and lemon rind (zest). Add three-quarters of beaten egg and mix well. Gradually add remaining egg until dough takes shape but is not too wet. If too sticky, add a little extra flour. Divide dough into three portions. Using your hands, roll each into a sausage shape about 3cm (1in) in diameter. Place rolls on baking sheets lined with baking parchment at least 6cm (2½in) apart. Lightly flatten. Bake about 20 minutes until golden brown. Remove from oven and leave for 10 minutes to cool and firm up.

Reduce oven temperature to 140C (275F/Gas 1). Using a serrated knife and cutting at an angle, cut each roll into very thin slices. Lay slices on baking sheets. Return them to the oven and cook for a further 10 minutes. Turn each biscotti over and cook for another 10 minutes. Remove from oven and cool on wire racks. Can be stored in airtight containers for up to 2 weeks. Serve with coffee, desserts, or soft cheeses.

*Can be Parev*
*Makes about 60*

# — DATE & BRANDY PUDDINGS —

350g (12oz) pitted dates, prunes or sultanas, finely
  chopped
5 tablespoons strong black coffee
6 tablespoons brandy
190g (6½oz) soft butter or margarine
350g (12oz/1¾ cups) caster (superfine) sugar
225g (8oz/2 cups) plain (all-purpose) flour
1 teaspoon bicarbonate of soda (baking soda)
4 eggs, lightly beaten
ZABAGLIONE SAUCE
1 teaspoon instant coffee
6 egg yolks
50g (2oz) caster (superfine) sugar
2 tablespoons Kahlua liqueur

To make the puddings, lightly grease
8 individual pudding bowls or 1 large bowl.
Combine fruit, coffee and brandy in a small
saucepan. Bring to a boil and simmer for
3 minutes. Reserve 3 tablespoons of cooking
liquid. Drain fruit and divide equally
between pudding bowls.

Cream butter and sugar together in a large
mixing bowl. Beat in flour, bicarbonate of
soda (baking soda), eggs and reserved
cooking liquid and mix well. Pour mixture
over fruit, filling each pudding bowl three-
quarters full.

Make foil circle(s) large enough to overlap top of each bowl by at least 2.5 cm (1in) and grease them. Secure a greased foil circle over each bowl using a rubber band. Place small pudding bowls in a deep frying pan (skillet) with a lid, or large bowl in a casserole. Add enough boiling water to come two-thirds up sides of bowl(s). Bring to a boil and simmer, covered, for 35 minutes for individual puddings or 1½ hours for large pudding. They are cooked when a skewer inserted comes out clean.

Meanwhile, make the zabaglione sauce about 15 minutes before pudding is ready. Mix instant coffee in 2 tablespoons hot water. Whisk coffee, egg yolks, sugar and Kahlua together in a food mixer. Transfer to a double-boiler or heat-proof bowl over a saucepan of simmering water. Whisk vigorously until the mixture has increased to four times its original volume and is pale and fluffy.

To serve, invert each puddings or place a slice of one large pudding on to a warm serving plate. Spoon some zabaglione sauce over and serve immediately.

*Can be Parev*
*Serves 8*

# - LIME MOUSSE WITH AMARETTI -

4 eggs, separated
225g (8oz/1¼ cups) caster (superfine) sugar
rind (zest) of 4 limes and juice of 3 limes
2 teaspoons cornflour (cornstarch) [potato flour for
  Pesach]
7g or 1 envelope gelatine dissolved in 4 tablespoons
  hot water
4 tablespoons white rum [supervised liqueur for
  Pesach] (optional)
300ml (10fl oz/1¼ cups) double (heavy) cream [or
  Parev whipping (heavy) cream]
200g (7oz) amaretti (macaroons), roughly crushed
2 limes, thinly sliced, to decorate

Combine egg yolks and sugar in a food
mixer until thick and pale; set aside.
Gradually mix lime juice with cornflour
(cornstarch). Stir in cooled gelatine. Cook
egg and gelatine mixtures in a deep
saucepan over a low heat, stirring
occasionally, for 15-20 minutes, until
thickened. Do not boil. Stir in
2 tablespoons of rum, if using, and lime rind
(zest). Cool for about 30 minutes. Whip
cream until just thick. Gradually whisk
remaining rum, if using, into cream. Using a
metal spoon, fold cream into custard.

Beat egg whites until stiff peaks form. Fold
1 tablespoon of egg white into lime mixture
using a metal spoon. Fold in remaining egg
whites in the same way. Spoon mousse into
large dessert or wine glasses and sprinkle
crushed amaretti on top. Leave to set for at
least 4 hours or overnight in the fridge.
Serve decorated with lime slices.

*Can be Parev. Pesach friendly*
*Serves 8-10*

# – PAREV HAZELNUT ICE-CREAM –

**PRALINE**
250g (9oz) skinned hazelnuts (filberts)
225g (8oz/1¼ cups) caster (superfine) sugar
**ICE CREAM**
550ml (20fl oz/2½ cups) soya cream
850ml (30fl oz/3¾ cups) sweetened soya milk
7 egg yolks
175g (6oz/¾ cup) caster (superfine) sugar
2 tablespoons cornflour (cornstarch)

Preheat the oven to 200C (400F/Gas 6).
Line a baking sheet with baking parchment.
Spread hazelnuts (filberts) in a single layer.

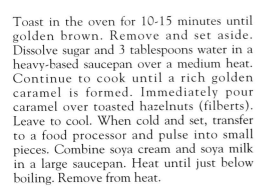

Toast in the oven for 10-15 minutes until golden brown. Remove and set aside. Dissolve sugar and 3 tablespoons water in a heavy-based saucepan over a medium heat. Continue to cook until a rich golden caramel is formed. Immediately pour caramel over toasted hazelnuts (filberts). Leave to cool. When cold and set, transfer to a food processor and pulse into small pieces. Combine soya cream and soya milk in a large saucepan. Heat until just below boiling. Remove from heat.

Whisk egg yolks and sugar until pale and thick. Add cornflour (cornstarch) and whisk briefly. Pour milk on to egg mixture and whisk together. Return to heat and cook over a low heat, stirring constantly. Do not boil. When mixture coats the back of spoon, pour into a bowl and cool for 30 minutes. Mix hazelnut praline into custard base and freeze in a suitable container for at least 4 hours. Remove from freezer about 30 minutes before serving.

*Serves 8-10*

# -CINNAMON TOAST & CHERRIES-

1 tablespoon arrowroot
2 x 375g (13oz) cans pitted cherries, 300ml
    (10fl oz/1¼ cups) juice reserved
2 tablespoons crème de cassis or Kiddush wine
cinnamon, for dusting
caster (superfine) sugar, for dusting
6 thick slices of cinnamon bread, brioche or challah
icing (confectioners') sugar, for dusting
550ml (20fl oz/2½ cups) ice cream of your choice
    [Parev for a meat meal]

Mix arrowroot with 2 tablespoons of the
cherry juice to form a thin paste. Add
remaining juice and crème de cassis.

Heat in a saucepan over a medium heat,
stirring continuously, until thickened. Add
cherries to the syrup and heat through. Dust
slices of bread in a mixture of cinnamon and
caster (superfine) sugar. Toast or grill (broil)
dusted bread.

Cut toast in half and place one half on a
warmed plate. Spoon 2 tablespoons of hot
cherries over. Place another slice of bread
on top at an angle. Add 1 more tablespoon
of cherries. Dust the plates with cinnamon
and icing (confectioners') sugar. Serve
immediately with scoops of ice-cream.

*Can be Parev*
*Serves 6*

# TOFFEE APPLE CRUMBLE

40g (1½oz/3 tablespoons) unsalted butter or
  margarine
50g (2oz/⅓ cup) dark soft brown sugar
6 tablespoons golden (corn) syrup
300ml (10fl oz/1¼ cups) double (heavy) cream [soya
  cream for Parev]
2-3 large cooking apples, peeled, cored and finely
  sliced
TOPPING
85g (3oz/⅔ cup) wholemeal flour
85g (3oz/¾ cup) plain (all-purpose) flour
50g (2oz/½ cup) rolled oats
85g (3oz/⅓ cup) butter or margarine
85g (3oz/½ cup) soft brown sugar
2 teaspoons cinnamon

Preheat the oven to 180C (350F/Gas 4).
Make the toffee sauce by heating butter or
margarine, dark soft brown sugar and golden
(corn) syrup in a small saucepan. Melt
completely and boil for 3 minutes until
golden brown. Remove from heat and stir in
cream, mixing well.

**Chef's Tip:** Before measuring out golden
(corn) syrup, dip the spoon into very hot
water to prevent the syrup sticking.

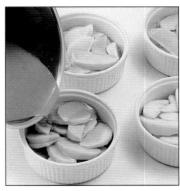

Put all the topping ingredients in a food
processor and pulse until the mixture
resembles breadcrumbs. Cover base of
8 individual ramekins or one large
ovenproof dish with sliced apples. Pour
toffee sauce over sliced apples, coating
thoroughly. Cover with topping mixture.
Bake for 30 minutes. Serve with ice-cream
or single (light) cream.

*Can be Parev*
*Serves 8-10*

# THIN PEAR PASTRIES

25g (1oz) skinned hazelnuts (filberts)
375g (13oz) ready-rolled puff pastry
2 egg yolks, beaten, for glazing
115g (4oz) marzipan
2-3 ripe dessert pears, thinly sliced
3 tablespoons icing (confectioners') sugar
apricot jam (preserve), for glazing

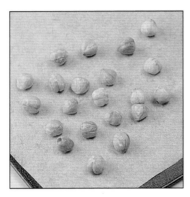

Preheat the oven to 200C (400F/Gas 6). Roast whole hazelnuts (filberts), for 10-15 minutes until toasted. Leave to cool. Line a baking sheet with baking parchment. Using a 12cm (4½in) cutter, cut 6 individual rounds from ready-rolled pastry.

Place pastry rounds on to a lined baking sheet. Glaze each round with beaten egg yolk. Put cooled hazelnuts (filberts) into a food processor and process until ground. Add marzipan to ground hazelnuts (filberts) in food processor and process to combine. Add 1 teaspoon water, drop by drop, until a soft paste forms. Divide the mixture into 6 and roll into balls. Place a ball in centre of each pastry round. Flatten ball with the palm of your hand to fill the centre of the round.

Place pear slices carefully on marzipan pastry rounds, leaving a 1cm (½in) pastry border all round. Sieve icing (confectioners') sugar over pastries. Bake for 15-20 minutes until golden brown. Remove from oven and cool. Melt and sieve apricot jam (preserve) to make a glaze. Brush each pastry with glaze. Serve with the hazelnut (filbert) ce-cream, Greek yogurt, cream or ice-cream.

*Can be Parev*
*Serves 6*

## ——————— PLUM TARTE TATIN ———————

150g (5oz/⅔ cup) caster (superfine) sugar
20 plums, halved (use half apricots if in season)
2 teaspoon ground mixed spice
flour, for dusting
450g (1lb) puff pastry
1 beaten egg yolk, for glazing

Preheat the oven to 220C (425F/Gas 7). Put sugar and 1 tablespoon water in a 25cm (10in) ovenproof frying pan (skillet). Arrange plums cut-side up to cover base of pan.

Fry over a medium heat for 15-20 minutes until the plums start to soften and sugar begins to caramelize. Remove from heat and drain off any excess juice. Sprinkle fruit evenly with ground mixed spice. On a lightly floured surface, roll puff pastry to a circle slightly larger than frying pan (skillet). Place pastry over frying pan (skillet) and tuck in round the edge. Glaze pastry with beaten egg yolk.

Bake for 20 minutes or until the pastry is golden. Remove and allow to cool for 5 minutes. Carefully drain off any excess juice if necessary. To turn out, cover pan with a large, deep serving plate and invert. Serve with Parev ice-cream or, if you are having a milk meal, then offer double (heavy) cream or vanilla ice-cream.

*Can be Parev*
*Serves 8*

# INDEX